A NOTE ABOUT THE AUTHOR

Michihiro Matsumoto was born in Osaka in 1940, and graduated from Kwansei Gakuin University. Before passing the toughest test for simultaneous translators given at the U.S. Embassy in Tokyo, he had founded and still leads a quarter-of-a-century-old school of English that combines language study with precepts of the martial arts, called *Eigo-do*. He has written more than sixty books on subjects ranging from the English language, cross cultural business communication, and a novel with a business background; he has also compiled a dictionary of modern Japanese-English colloquialisms, with Edward Seidensticker, the renowned translator of *The Tale of Genji*.

THE UNSPOKEN WAY

HARAGEI:
Silence in Japanese Business and Society

Michihiro Matsumoto

KODANSHA INTERNATIONAL
Tokyo • New York • London

Distributed in the United States by Kodansha America, Inc., 114 Fifth Avenue, New York, N.Y. 10011, and in the United Kingdom and continental Europe by Kodansha Europe Ltd., Gillingham House, 38-44 Gillingham Street, London SW1V 1HU. Published by Kodansha International Ltd., 17-14 Otowa 1-chome, Bunkyo-ku, Tokyo 112, and Kodansha America, Inc.
Originally published in Japanese in 1984, under the title *HARAGEI*, by Kodansha Ltd.
First edition, 1988
92 93 94 95 5 4 3

LCC 88-80138
ISBN 0-87011-889-7 (U.S.)
ISBN 4-7700-1389-2 (in Japan)

CONTENTS

PREFACE

Frustrated Western journalists in Japan look upon this country as a cohesive, close-knit society. Cultural anthropologists regard Japan as a high-context culture where so much is shared amongst Japanese that there is very little need for them to rely on verbal communication. Pragmatic Western businessmen see Japan as a success story in the business world and believe that they can learn from its management practice because it has "worked." Americans, basically uninformed about Japan except for its exports: TV sets, cars, cameras, etc., see *Shogun* on television or read *The Ninja* and come away puzzled at the enigmatic nature of the Japanese. A horde of individually unobtrusive Japanese businessmen, not to mention seemingly nonvenomous MBA candidates, keep coming to the United States. And like it or not, an image has been forged of Asian "insects" playing havoc with crops on U.S. soil. One significant result—an enraged U.S. Congress and subsequent "insecticidal" and punitive trade bills.

Still, in the minds of the American people, these basic questions remain: Who are the Japanese? Have they ever defined themselves? How have they managed to rise to international prominence without defining themselves? Has *Time* Magazine done justice to the Japanese, in its well-documented special issue on Japan (Aug. 1, 1983), when it labelled Japan, "A Nation in Search of Itself?" The truth of the matter is that Japan is *also* a nation *not* in search of itself.

This may lead Westerners to suspect that the Japanese have an entirely different set of guiding principles by which they operate. The seemingly outrageous statement by Professor Chie Nakane of Tokyo University, that the "Japanese have no principles" (*Newsweek*) was assuredly shocking to many Western readers and at the same time reinforced their conjecture that, yes, something *is* different about the Japanese. A notable example was the unexpected resignation in 1987 of the top executives of Toshiba, parent company of the beleaguered Toshiba Machinery Co.

Toshiba was severely criticized for exporting an item prohibited by COCOM (Coordinating Committee for Export Control to Communist Areas) to the Soviet Union. The resignation was simply an indication of the executives assuming responsibility for the condemned act, a culturally appropriate response to such a burden of responsibility.

What makes the Japanese tick? Evidence shows that the Japanese do not seem to possess principles, if the word *principle* is to be defined from the logic-oriented Western perspective. Logic is considered to be "cold" or "unemotional" in Japan and certainly not identical to the truth. By contrast, *kimochi* (emotions) or *omoiyari* (caring), being "warm," are more likely to be used to avoid situations of conflict. If neither is used, a case can be made that the Japanese are not motivated by the mind or the heart alone, but by the *hara*: a primordial center both in man and nature.

Hara is hardly logic; but it has a logic of its own. *Haragei* is the art of using one's *hara* in interpersonal communication. Is *haragei* a monopoly of Japanese culture? Many Japanese claim it is. But can they define it verbally? The average Japanese's immediate gut reaction: "It's tough even for Japanese to explain it in words. It takes a Japanese to understand *haragei*. If you can't feel it, it proves you're a *gaijin* (non-Japanese)."

Embarrassment came some ten years ago when I was asked the following unprompted question by Sen Nishiyama, then head of simultaneous interpreting at the American Embassy (and former advisor to Sony): "It's widely accepted that Saigo Takamori and Katsu Kaishu engaged in *haragei* to bring about the bloodless surrender of Edo (Tokyo) Castle. But recently Eto Jun, a noted critic, refuted this common belief by saying it was far from being *haragei*, because vital information had already been flowing back and forth between the military leaders secretly. What is your opinion?"

I was stunned. The embarrassment was threefold. One, a Japanese never asks a question about *haragei*. *Haragei* is understood tacitly in Japan—hardly a topic for discussion. Two, a master rarely asks such an obvious question of his disciple in Japan. (At that time I was a student of simultaneous interpreting under, and not with, him at the United States Information Service of the American Embassy.) Three, I simply didn't know the answer. The episode was so taken for granted in Japan that I had not really given it any serious thought.

The bilingual master's unexpected question inspired me to take on the task of unraveling the myth of *haragei*: that it cannot be analyzed or described, let alone be explained to anyone—Japanese or non-Japanese.

In attempting to dispel the diehard myths about *haragei*, I am caught on the horns of a dilemma. How can I make *haragei* more easily understood by non-Japanese readers, who were brought up to demand clarity and purpose in writing, without losing Japanese readers who expect me to preserve the mystic quality of *haragei*.

Torn between two value systems which are poles apart, I have decided to have it both ways: clarity and obscurity, without, I hope, losing either type of reader. I am truly indebted to many persons whom I have relied upon for help or insights, including journalists, scholars, businessmen, editors (more than ten), and critical listeners of my lectures on *haragei* over the past ten years. Not a single one of the sixty books I have written in Japanese, not even a dictionary I jointly compiled with associates, has caused me more time, money, effort, and frustration.

My unquenchable thirst for the cultural parallel of *haragei* in other countries and within other cultures has brought me to the study of the Jews. For reasons which I attempt to elucidate in various parts of this book, theirs seems to be a culture and has been an historical experience which appears to be the diametrical opposite of the Japanese.

The only way fish can define themselves as animals living in the water is for them to get out of the water. By the same token, the shortest route to giving *haragei* clarity is to shed light on a culture whose self-understanding and representation seems to be so different from the Japanese. The Jewish people's struggle with the definition of identity, still such an ambiguous notion, is untranslatable into Japanese.

The Jewish people, devoid of the historical parallel of the divine wind (*Kamikaze*) keeping a people from wandering, being scattered, has never had the mutual indulgence (*Amae*) the idealistic Japanese race has enjoyed. The awareness that brings the Jews together seems to be based on some reality principle, in Freudian terms, by no means the sort of pleasure principle that "laughs at" debates about survival.

Haragei, the opposite of debate or directed discussion, may defy logic as a tool of thinking but accepts it when the spirit moves the author to probe the otherwise non-assertive emotions of an "unchosen people."

Haragei is the product of the culture of Japan which in turn is the product of its unparalleled history of several thousand years of *non-wandering*. To discuss *haragei* is to put into perspective the psyche of the Japanese, who have never had a compelling reason to burn their bridges behind them for the survival of their entire race.

Even the International Tribunal of War Criminals (known as the Tokyo Trials) gave only the War Criminals death by hanging, yet failed even by victor's justice to make the entire Japanese race morally responsible for their patriotic war that engulfed the whole nation. Who among the Japanese verbally asked *why*? Who has wondered *aloud* if they themselves were proven guilty by the Western sense of justice? Who knows, they may have "stomached" away their mixed emotions in their art of tranquility maintenance. Someone who did speak out was of course not Japanese, but the Indian Justice Radha Binode Pal, who argued vehemently that the Japanese War Criminals should not be prosecuted. Right or wrong is not exactly the question.

The Japanese, who viscerally understand both sides of justice by being unable to logically express their "*hara*", have chosen to remain silent and outwardly optimistic; likewise the troops of those non-assertive and non-argumentative Japanese business-men who are now "terrorizing" the U.S. economy.

The possible questions Jews, Orthodox or non-Orthodox, ask themselves before they make decisions are: Why was I born Jewish? Why am I growing up Jewish? Why will I die Jewish? What if I were not born Jewish? Why should I grow up Jewish? Why should I die Jewish? Is there any reason why I should stay Jewish? Why, why, why and an equal number of why-nots. Have Japanese asked themselves why they are Japanese? The very absence of "why" questions seems to make Japanese unique and different from the rest of the world. What other logic can explain an enig-matic quality of their behavior other than the logic of *hara*? An attempt to demythologize the uniqueness of Japanese *hara* for me is both adventure and romance. It is the driving force responsible for my renewed determination, spurred on by Kodansha Interna-tional to revise the earlier version of *HARAGEI*. Chapters have been added and hopefully along the way some more enlightened perspectives have been gained as a result of numerous dealings with non-Japanese in business, academia, and the media in over thirty countries.

Michihiro Matsumoto

INTRODUCTION

Writing an introduction to *Haragei* poses a dilemma which illustrates both the need for the book and one of the problems it raises. The dilemma is: who is the reader? Is he Japanese or Western? If he is of European cultural heritage, a member of one of those families of cultures now referred to as Western, then the author comes right to the point by using a low-context, linear approach. If, on the other hand, the reader is Japanese, the author must avoid the obvious and say more about the situation—the context or setting of the book. It is as though one part of the world focused its attention on the message, with little regard to context, while the other part did just the opposite. Clearly both must be taken into account. Stated somewhat differently, it is as though the Western cultures emphasize the left side of the brain, thereby enhancing the linearity of Western languages, while the Japanese make much more use of the right hemisphere of the cerebral cortex. Having been reared in the context of Western cultures, I have chosen the more linear approach on the assumption that Japanese readers will benefit from the practice they receive when exposed to the writings of the Western mind, while the Western readers can start with a few steps taken on familiar ground before they venture further into the new subject of *haragei*. Our topic is actually intercultural communication in the context of Japanese and Western cultures, but most specifically Japanese and American cultures.

At first glance, few people realize that there is even a problem in translating from one culture to the next. However, with time and experience the Westerner eventually comes face-to-face with the sticky *natto* (fermented soybeans) of Japanese society. Even in Europe, where people have been living next to each other, interacting, trading, and enjoying one another's literature and music for centuries, the blockages to successful intercultural communication are not only real, but, on close examination, frequently prove to be virtually insoluble. Throughout the world, cultural differences are of the same genre: for example, do people depend more on legal agreements or on trusting other human beings? This is not just an academic matter, but one that cuts to the core of life. If you can't trust someone in a culture that is built on trust, then how do you operate? There are literally hundreds of small but basic and important differences of this sort.

An American friend who is the third generation of his family to have lived in Japan, and who is fluent not only in the language but the culture as well, used to keep a file of crucial bits of cultural "know-how" that Westerners must master if they are to deal successfully with the Japanese. He only included things that, unknown, would inevitably lead to disillusionment, distrust, economic ruin, or complete breakdown in communication. Five years after beginning the list he was still discovering new items almost daily! Some of this stems from the highly situational character of Japanese life, the rules changing from situation to situation, a point made by Matsumoto. Also, the critical situations lie predominantly in those aspects of life which people take most for granted and which are therefore not spelled out. The fact that each culture has its own inventory of crucial behaviors and responses does not simplify matters. What one culture takes for granted, the next one deals with in a highly technical manner. For anyone working in the intercultural field, one of the cardinal principles is that each culture must be approached anew, with a fresh eye to the nuances and subtleties that communicate true meaning in any transaction.

For example, in the United States, when addressing one's colleagues one takes it for granted not only that they have read something one has written, but that one's political and philosophical positions have little relevance to one's approach to scientific matters. This is not true in Italy, as I once learned to my distress when addressing a group of colleagues in Rome. In Italy, unless one begins with some sort of statement as to where one is in the political spectrum of left to right and unless there is a statement of one's philosophical antecedents, the audience may have difficulty relating to what you are saying. In the United States, it is an unwritten rule that one will compartmentalize one's politics and one's science, keeping them uncontaminated by each other. Nor do we start with the assumption that we will be attacked and that the audience is there in part to make as much personal gain as possible at the speaker's expense. We, in the United States, usually try to keep a civil tongue in our heads, whether it be a formal lecture or simply an informal discussion between peers. The French do not; instead they use a "no holds barred" approach that is frequently distressing to Americans. In a debate in the U.S., each side is responsible for the accuracy of its own facts. In Great Britain it is one's opponents' facts that one is responsible for! The result is that English academicians have the impression that Americans are naive and uneducated because many of them remain silent while the English make increasingly outlandish statements, waiting for their American audience to challenge them—something the Americans could have done all along but were too polite to do to a guest in their country. These examples are relatively superficial and scientists surmount them daily; but they are illustrative of the type of thing that can happen even between closely related cultures. How then does one approach the matter of intercultural relationships, knowing that the rules may not only be different but that many of the crucial differences have not been written down or described? Part of the answer is in the matter of approach—or how the problem is defined.

Almost a quarter of a century ago, I put forth the idea that culture is really a metacommunication system. Not only words have meaning; everything else has meaning as well. How one handles appointments and obligations in time constitutes a message, as does one's behavior as a member of one's own sex. How one learns is itself a communication to others. In the United States we ask questions. In Japan you avoid questions. Think for a minute what a difference this one single item can make and how anxiety-provoking it would be to someone who sincerely wanted to know, if they were forced to forego asking questions? The Japanese have been brought up to avoid coming to the point too quickly. In fact, the point may only be alluded to indirectly or in a few lines of *haiku*. The result is that the Japanese are past masters at reading between the lines. Americans are just the opposite. They get anxious when they don't know what someone else is driving at. They are taught to get to the point quickly—hence the suspense of the detective story where our need for closure is tantalizingly frustrated until the very end. All of these things and hundreds more have meaning, but the meaning is unique to each culture. It is all part of how life is lived and experienced, what is worthwhile and what is not, how one works with colleagues and fits into a group, and how one advances and why one does not. It dictates the moral implications of different acts: whether one is tormented by guilt or reduced to humbleness in shame for past acts; whether one gets a contract or not, or if one retains or fails to keep it. All of life's strategies imply and are supported on a foundation of unwritten, taken-for-granted rules and assumptions. All are necessary for survival and a challenge to understand, but with all this difficulty, what a wonderful, diverse world it is that we live in!

One of the hazards of chasing the will-o'-the-wisp of cultural understanding is that most of what is written is for the members of the writer's own culture, all taking the same things for granted. Practically nothing is written about this little-known area of taken-for-granted behavior. Matsumoto's book is one of the rare exceptions. His insights are reinforced by specific Japanese terms that express key philosophical and cultural points in Japan. His notion of the art of *hara* is important to those of us in the West who want to understand Japan, because in *haragei* one finds a key operating principle to be followed by anyone who wishes to be a successful communicator in Japan.

Whether there is anything quite like *haragei* in the West is as yet undetermined. My own hunch is that since the Japanese fall into what I term the "high context" group of cultures—those that are homogenous, where it is not necessary to cross every "t" and dot every "i" to be understood—and since *haragei* is a direct out-growth of the high-context setting in which not just the words but the pattern of silences—*ma*—has meaning, the few parallels to be found in the West will be highly specific ones where the meaning is quite restricted. Matsumoto has done us all a service in writing this book.

Edward T. Hall
Santa Fe, New Mexico

GLOSSARY OF JAPANESE TERMS

Amae
A psychological dependence on the good will of others, sometimes understood as mutual help or sympathy. The kind of symbiotic relationship that exists between parent and child for example, which does not seem to require any rational or logical justification or explanation, is often used as an example that imparts the feeling or atmosphere of this term. In Japanese the pictographic symbol [甘え] used in the word *amae* is also used to express the following related terms: *amaeru*—to coax, and *kangen*—flattery.

Giri and *Ninjo*
Giri and *Ninjo* are different facets of the same sphere of behavior having to do with the handling of debts or obligations (in the widest sense). *Giri* has to do with the dutiful fulfillment of moral obligation, whether or not a formal agreement exists. *Ninjo* is connected more with the nature of feelings or sympathy governing the extent of the burden of duty implied by *giri*. In the absence of written rules and laws, traditional Japanese society relied on these principles to maintain order and maintain peace among the members of the community. Common expressions using these concepts include: *ninjo-mi-no-aru-hito* (kindhearted person) *giri-gatai-hito* (consistently, responsibly fulfilling all obligations).

Hara
Literally meaning belly or guts (as in *harakiri*, suicide by cutting the belly), this word's significance as a concept involves connotations connected in the West with heart, mind, soul, intuition and feeling; it might more accurately be described as a combination of all these and more.

Haragei
Literally meaning the art or practice of using *hara*, this is a concept which this book, *THE UNSPOKEN WAY*, endeavors to explore. It refers, in one simple sense, to a visceral communication among Japanese that defies Western logic.

Honne and *Tatemae*
These terms are often used as contrasting yet complementary parts of a whole, *honne* being understood as being related to the private, true self, and *tatemae* typifying the public persona and behavior. *Honne* then has to do with real intentions and sincere feelings, while *tatemae* conveys the face the world sees.

Ishin Denshin
Intuitive understanding, without use of words or signs; a peculiarly Japanese form of telepathic communication, as a result of some intimate relationship or bond.

Kao
Literally meaning face, this often indicates not only a person's physical appearance, but also his sense of honor and self respect; much of the application of *haragei* is involved with the awareness of the need to save face.

Kokoro
A term that, as in other cultures, not only means heat, but also has connotations of feeling, emotion and spirituality.

Ma
A space or interval, either in the physical sense or in the sense of a pause in conversation which, by its existence, expresses meaning as much as a spoken word; an important concept in Japanese non-verbal communication.

Michi
Michi is written with the same character as the Chinese word *tao*, and similarly means road or path, both in the sense of street and in the philosophical sense of Way, or Guide to Enlightenment. In Japanese the character is sometimes pronounced *dō*, as in judo, karate-do or kendo.

Nemawashi
Related to the preliminary stages of reaching an agreement prior to formal discussions or negotiations; the building up of a consensus so that the eventual agreement is a foregone conclusion.

Oyabun and *Kobun*
Oyabun is the father figure of a group or organization, whose relationship with subordinates, or *kobun*, is based as much on their mutual, unspoken loyalty as on any chain of command or formal organizational structure.

Sunao
Obedience to the general will; subordination of one's own individual feelings to those of a larger group.

I

WHAT IS *HARAGEI?*

A.   Conflicting definitions of *haragei*

1.   *Haragei* is all things to all people

Haragei, which I consider to be the last bastion of Japanese uniqueness, is the art of belly or abdomen, if translated literally. Sample definitions from Japanese to English dictionaries include: psychological acting; acting on the strength of one's personality; a psychological game; a plucky act; a belly art; etc, etc, etc. But none of these definitions seems to do full justice to the reality of *haragei* as it occurs.

The essence of *haragei*, however, is more closely described in this definition given by one of the most authoritative Japanese dictionaries, *Jikai*:

1) the verbal or physical action one employs to influence others by the potency of rich experience and boldness;
2) the act of dealing with people or situations through ritual formalities and accumulated experience.

Karlfried Dürckheim, in *Hara, The Vital Center of Man*, unveils the mystery of this art as he defines it "precisely the ability of 'Nature' to express itself completely unhindered by the limitations of the five senses and the intellect." These two definitions seem either too descriptive or too cosmic for the layman to comprehend.

Resultant confusion can be justified. For if you ask a hundred people to define *haragei*, you are likely to be confronted with a hundred different definitions. The following are excerpts from the interviews I conducted and the books I have read:

High school student:
"I often see the word in print, but I don't know what it is."

College co-ed:
"A belly dance? A form of entertainment at a stag party?"

College boy:
"*Haragei* is the game they play in society—you don't disagree, you don't argue."

Young office worker:
"A dirty game politicans play—mutual back-scratching, you know?"

Middle-aged American expert on Kabuki:
"Kabuki is *haragei*. You watch a Kabuki performance from your *hara*, not from your mind or heart."

Young journalist:
"*Haragei* is beyond logic. What could I say to an old man with a solid reputation who greeted me at the door in total nudity? It was appalling. On second thought, that was genuine *haragei*."

Middle-aged businessman:
"The name of the game in Japan is *haragei*—situational ethics, pragmatism before ideology."

Old man:
"*Haragei* reminds me of Jutaro Komura, a Meiji-born diplomat. Once he was late for an appointment with a foreign dignitary aboard a ship. Before climbing the steps, he deliberately broke his gold watch, a treasured gift from his honored teacher. He proceeded to blame the watch for his tardiness—without actually apologizing and thus losing face. That's beautiful *haragei* acting. Why? I don't know."

Liberated American woman:

"If it's true that it is a characteristic or ability peculiar to the Japanese male, then it is most likely male chauvinism."

Englishman who had spent twenty frustrating years in Japan:

"Now I know Japan is all *haragei. Haragei* is the "open sesame" to the enigma of the Japanese culture."

Old politician:

"*Haragei* doesn't work any longer, because we have no unselfishly motivated *haragei* practitioners these days. And I'm sad. Consensus-forming calls for 'art' not 'technique'. *Haragei* is not gamesmanship."

Western journalist:

"The reason the Japanese government refuses to accept refugees is that they fear that their *haragei* tradition will break down."

Author of *How to Get People To Do Things*:

"Empathy is being able to feel as the other person feels. *Haragei* is the art of getting within the other person."

Non-Japanese editor of my *Haragei* articles:

"*Haragei* is the art of (subtly) presenting the other guy with options."

Former KDD official in New York:

"Americans trust paper (contracts), but we Japanese don't. Instead we rely on kin-tract (kinship-contract) based on *haragei.*"

Member of Liberal Democratic Party:

"There is good *haragei* and bad *haragei*. Bad *haragei* must be eliminated while good *haragei* must survive. *Haragei* is intrinsic to Japanese politics. Debate, however, must be the wave of the future.

Author of *Japan's Decision To Surrender*:

"A man who 'uses' *haragei* is a man who says one thing but means another."

Korean professor:

"Even if a Japanese can practice *haragei*, unless he is capable of intuiting what others are thinking, he will not succeed. He expects others to read between the lines, rather than have things spelled out. Those who can neither make themselves understood nor intuit what others are really thinking will never be trusted as more than half a man. That is a very Japanese way of thinking."

Professor at International Christian University:

"*Haragei* is the least confrontational form of negotiation."

Author of *Shadows of the Rising Sun*:

"An actor's ability to express his feelings directly to his audience without saying or doing anything."

All this proves is that *haragei* means all things to all people. Indeed, this variety of interpretation is a testimony to the scope of *haragei*.

2. Is *haragei* a game?

The word game is relatively easy to define. Eric Berne, author of a one-time bestseller, *Games People Play*, defines a game as an ongoing series of complementary ulterior transactions progressing to a well-defined, predictable outcome. He further asserts: "Games are clearly differentiated from procedures, rituals, and pastimes by two chief characteristics: (1) their ulterior quality; (2) the pay off. Procedures may be successful, rituals effective, and pastimes profitable, but all of them are by definition candid; they may involve contest, but not conflict, and the ending may be sensational, but it is not dramatic. Every game, on the other hand, is basically dishonest, and the outcome has a dramatic, as distinct from merely exciting, quality."

By this definition, *haragei* is not a game. *Haragei*, though it does have a pragmatic and gamy aspect, should not be confused with game-playing. The success in "clean" *haragei* lies in the candidness of the participants. Their *hara*, by definition, are clean and pure—this is the first prerequisite to bringing about clean *haragei*. Since the essential quality of *hara* is circular, friend and enemy are not mutually exclusive but complementary in a circular way. By this line of circular reasoning, we are our enemy's enemy to be conquered first. Conquering ourselves is definitely not game-playing.

Second, *haragei* is essentially a ritual. The only official criterion of its success, if any, is effectiveness in reaching consensus, and never efficiency in rendering decisions, because the pay-off has to be kept private. Participants do not "play" a ritual; they just perform it.

Third, *haragei* has elements of play, since it is drama on stage or off stage. It has to be enjoyed to the extent that the fun-motivated audience identifies with actors (not just a single good guy, but bad guys as well) in the real-life drama.

Kaishu Katsu, a military strategist and a well-known *haragei* performer, had this to say on negotiations: "Things don't work out the way I expect. So I usually don't think and plan ahead. I just get all thoughts out; that's why I can negotiate according to the situation. Don't play games." To *haragei* negotiators, the pay-off, procedures, and time are also negotiable. Their unending faith and uncompromising principle remain one: the only constant is change. How can *haragei* participants be called game players when their goal is both-of-us-win (never I-must-win) and the rules of the game—and the game itself—are subject to change?

Haragei is a center-to-center communication as below:

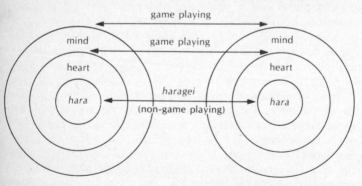

Figure 1 *Haragei* is non-game playing

3. *Haragei* misunderstood

A non-Japanese friend of mine insisted that *haragei* was a universal phenomenon and not restricted to Japanese. His argument was based on the way Jesus Christ handled an angry crowd shouting murderous phrases in front of the temple gate. The object of the crowd's wrath was a young woman who was caught in the act of adultery. The consequence of such an act, according to the law of Moses, was death by stoning. Jesus stood by the side of the woman and then stooped down and wrote on the ground with his finger. He raised himself and then repeated what he had written, "He that is without sin among you, let him cast the first stone." Again he stooped and traced some words with his finger as the crowd began to disperse. When he looked up all had departed except for the woman.

Jesus, my friend contended, executed an exquisite *haragei* performance that ended with everyone winning: Jesus teaching, the woman living and the crowd learning. True *haragei*? No. Let me explain why.

The Pharisees and Scribes were taunting Jesus to see if he believed he was above Moses' law. Thus, Jesus rectified the situation by thinking logically. This logical turn-the-tables method is a debater's own. Jesus, super-debater, was successful in winning the hearts and minds of the audience. Jesus was clearly the winner. He was an able rhetorician, unlike most harageists. And most importantly, Jesus thought and acted independently while harageists act dependently or interdependently. Harageists, despite the fact they usually feel on their own, seldom think on their own.

How would a harageist have acted? A harageist, totally unarmed, comes out of the crowd and says, "Kill me first." A silence. "I know she slept with many men," he continues, "I'm one of them. So I deserve your punishment." Then a burly man with knife in hand approaches the harageist and is ready to kill. The two men gaze steadfastly at one another, until the man lowers his knife and turns away: a meeting of the *hara*.

A debater's logic is essential for defining vague concepts. But can straight logic get the definition of *haragei* straight? Let me try.

Haragei, the opposite of straightforward communication and intrinsic to a close-knit society, is basically a game-free game, which has a few simple guidelines:

1) to yield to intuition (non-linear), rather than to intellectualization (linear)
2) to be more effectively enacted through effortless stylization rather than through the effort to appear natural
3) to be utilized by men in the later seasons of life (autumn or winter) with practical experience, rather than by principled ideologists, uncompromising religionists or committed moral leaders
4) to be performed at the level of *hara*, rather than that of heart or mind
5) to be more clearly identified in a confrontational setting where the interpersonal communication is based on "breath length," and to be tacitly (not necessarily nonverbally) performed with appropriate *ma* (pregnant pause), rather than verbally with precise language.

The above definition is almost uncontestable but made more elusive. The confusion arising from the structured definition can easily lend itself to the misunderstanding of the very nature of *haragei*.

4. *Haragei* by example

a. Kantaro Suzuki's *haragei*

What is a typical *haragei*? Well-informed scholars are reminded of a mysterious action by 79-year-old, then Japanese prime minister, Kantaro Suzuki, who strongly advocated the continuation of desperate war efforts with clenched fists but concealed his *"hara"* (unspoken belief: Japan's surrender) with sealed mouth.

His high-pitched argument for continued war efforts at the Imperial Conference "deluded" everyone present, including the Emperor of Japan. His *haragei* "deceived" the critics, the press, citizens, the Russians jealous of Japanese territory, thus saving Japan from national suicide. It worked. It created an emotional climate favorable for the Imperial decisions: Japan's surrender accepting unconditionally the Potsdam ultimatum in August, 1945. His lie was too big to be called a lie, and too big a truth, for that matter, to be called the truth. His *haragei* eventually deceived an American scholar Robert J. C. Butow, author of *Japan's Decision to Surrender*, who misinterprets *haragei*, by saying a man who uses *haragei* is a man who says one thing but means another.

Suzuki's action was genuine *haragei*. A man who uses *haragei* says one thing and quite another and means both. Suzuki's *haragei* is now "romanticized" and a *haragei* man can still get away with this sort of acting (not game playing). One of my stock definitions of *haragei* is the art of influencing others on the strength of one's personality or self-effacing acts rather than on the validity of his arguments.

b. Banboku Ohno's *haragei*
Since language is divisive rather than relational by nature, hara-gei negotiators minimize verbal exchanges in favor of "wordy" silence or *ma* (pauses pregnant with meaning). Since it is the *ma* that transcends the limited dualities of language, the art of syn-chronized breathing as well as *hara*-reading works in *hara*-to-*hara*-negotiations.

The late Banboku Ohno, a Meiji-born man of *hara* recommend-ed to the then Prime Minister Shigeru Yoshida that his friend, Kikuichiro Yamaguchi, be admitted into his Cabinet. The Prime Minister Yoshida had said, "No way," because he and Yamaguchi were not on the same breath-length. Aware that all the behind-the-scenes negotiations had failed, Ohno at his wits' end ven-tured to negotiate one-on-one with the prime minister. Ohno felt like he was talking to a brick wall, so after taking a long *ma* he began to chant *naniwabushi* (a heart-rending ballad), and putting himself farther out on a limb. "Masculinity... is not the only proof of a man... emotions and sentiments also..."

No sooner did Prime Minister Yoshida let down his guard and smile for the first time, than Ohno directly reasoned with

Yoshida. "Prime Minister, it is wise, isn't it, to keep the tiger in the cage? It would be unwise of you to turn the fierce tiger loose." The prime minister nodded affirmatively with a broader smile. The birth of a Cabinet minister, according to the provider of the above episode, was thus brought about by Ohno's *haragei*.

c. Miki Nakayama's quasi-haragei
Though I have already indicated and repeatedly insinuated at the risk of losing female readers that it is much tougher for women to develop *hara* than men, it does not mean women are not capable of *haragei* or a stunt resembling *haragei*.

An example is Miki Nakayama, foundress of Tenri-kyo, the biggest school of new religions.

Miki, as a hard-working wife, was late in having a child. This weighed heavily on the minds of her family members, justifiably. About that time, a maid-servant named Kano was in favor with her master, Zenbei. She took advantage of her position and grew more presumptuous each day, until one day the ambitious maid served Miki a bowl of poisoned soup, with a hope of stepping into her place by doing away with her.

Miki ate the soup and felt violent pain. But she was immediately taken care of. When the family discovered that she had been poisoned due to the intrigue of their own maid, they were infuriated.

But Miki spoke to them with labored breathing, "This is nothing but cleansing of my stomach by the gods and the Buddha."

At this, the family was petrified. The maid-servant awoke for the first time from her dream of delusion, deeply touched by Miki's generous heart, and expressed her profound regret for what she had done. She repented truly from the bottom of her heart and, in due course, departed from the Nakayama household, leaving their service of her own accord. ("The Life of *Oyasama*, Foundress of Tenrikyo," p. 13)

Her stomach-cleansing, whether she wanted it herself or not, helped others clean their stomachs, as it turned out.

Given this episode, it would not surprise readers to learn that when the arresting police came to put her under arrest, she instructed her followers to treat them politely with sweets and tea and said to the police officers with a graceful smile: "I've been expecting you, sir." Her *hara* acting, if not *haragei* per se, won her not only the hearts and minds, but the *hara* (stomach) of many a loyal follower, male and female.

B. Analysis of *haragei*

1. *Hara*

The literal meaning of *hara* is simply "stomach," located near the middle of our body and considered a vital center of our health and well-being. *Hara* is a point in our body which gives us mental and physical balance. *Hara* is man's contact with nature; or rather, *hara* is nature within our body. Traditionally it has been believed that the *hara* housed the spirit of courage, integrity, purity, flexibility, and *mushin* (or "no-mind"). The absence of mind gives rise to *ishin-denshin* (heart-to-heart interaction), which will be proven later to be the quintessence of Japanese art and a building block of *haragei*. It is this metaphysical meaning of *hara* that is subject to varied interpretations and misinterpretations. To give *hara* a clearer identity, let me offer my adaptation and extension of an oft-told Jewish joke.

Five Jewish intellectuals discussed in heaven the essence of life. Moses said, "The essence of life is in your head." Jesus Christ said, "No, Moses, you're wrong. What's most important in life is this," pointing to his heart. Karl Marx said, "You're both wrong. The most important thing in life is here . . . the stomach." Sigmund Freud said, "Gentlemen, you're all mistaken. The most important thing is further below the belt." And Albert Einstein said, "You are all completely off the mark. Everything is relative."

My joke does not end here. Put a Japanese participant in and we will get a multi-sided perspective on the situation. The Japanese intellectual kept silent, while smiling enigmatically and nodding in assent all the time. Erik Erikson, in the capacity of discussion leader, asked the Japanese, "What is your view?"

"Oooh, everyone's view," was the reply.

"Pardon?"

"Aaah, what they feel is what I feel."

"But everyone has a different argument."

"They're all the same to me."

"What makes you think their opinions are the same?"

"Because they are all thinking in their head."

"What's wrong with thinking in the head?"

"Such thinking gives rise to 'yes' or 'no.'"

"What do you mean?"

"The essence of life is not 'yes' or 'no' but 'yes *and* 'no.' If you think in terms of 'yes' or 'no,' you'll lose the most important thing."

"And what is the most important thing?"

"*Hara.*"

"What is *hara* . . . mind or heart?"

"They are both part of *hara*. When *hara* is given rational definition, it is no longer *hara*."

a. Hara *in the Japanese language*
The fact that a country does not have a word for *hara* does not prove that the people of the country do not have *hara*. Mexican gurus (like Don Juan) may possess it, assuming Castaneda's books have any authenticity. An excerpt:

> "There is a gap in us, like the soft spot on the head of a child which closes with age; this gap opens as one develops one's will."
>
> "Where is that gap?"
>
> "At the place of your luminous fibers," he said, pointing to his abdominal area.
>
> "What is it like? What is it for?"
>
> "It's an opening. It allows a space for the will to shoot out, like an arrow."
>
> (Carlos Castaneda, *A Separate Reality*, page 47)

However, a case can be made, I believe, that the phrases and idioms, including the word *hara*, are rich in the Japanese language—an indication that the users of the language set higher store on *hara*-oriented values.

I still remember my amazement when, in my early efforts to penetrate into the nature of the various Japanese "master practices" (first, in talks with a master of their arts) I heard again and again the word *hara* propounded with particular emphasis. Whenever I talked to a master of swordsmanship, of dancing, of puppetry, of painting, or of any other art, he invariably concluded his exposition of the relevant training by emphasizing *hara* as the cardinal point of all effort. Thus I soon realized that this word obviously meant more than a mere prerequisite for the unfailing exercise of any technique. *Hara* seemed to be connected with something fundamental, something ultimate. (Karlfried Dürckheim, *Hara: The Vital Center of Man*, page 37)

Haruo Yamaoka, a Buddhist priest, discusses *hara* in the introduction to his book titled *Meditation Gut Enlightenment*:

"Living with immigrant Japanese parents, I encountered many references to *hara*. It wasn't until I went to study in Japan, however, that I realized the meaning of my parents' continued reference to this particular area of their anatomy. The Japanese way of life focuses on *hara*. One may even call it their philosophy of life. Their way of *hara* takes in much of the social, physical, and psychological life of the Japanese, and it brings them calmness, stability, power, and flexibility." (pages 1–2)

Observing the fact that, in the East, the center of gravity is not located in the head as in the West, but in the lower belly (*hara*), Albert Low, author of *Zen and Creative Management* (Playboy) claims:

"Thus, locating the energies and attention in *hara* is not only of value to the martial artist but is also of equal value to the

31

businessman, who no less needs to be as responsive and incisive and who no less needs to use wisely his vital forces."

And I say, Amen. Businessmen, as I will explain later, do need *hara*.

I have travelled fairly extensively to various cities of the world and have talked to many people in search of their cultural parallel for *hara*, but the efforts ended in futility. The richness of *hara*-related words, as revealed in the following list, will be embarrassingly descriptive of the Japanese penchant for *hara* in their daily communication.

Vocabulary list of "hara-expressions"

HARA LANGUAGE	LITERAL TRANSLATION	CULTURAL TRANSLATION
Hara	Belly, abdomen, stomach	heart, courage, vital body center, real intentions, true motives
Hara-no-ookii-hito	a man of big *hara*	a generous person, a big-hearted person, usually a man with charisma
Hara-no-chiisai-hito	a man of small *hara*	a selfish person, an overly cautious and unforgiving person
Hara-no-dekita-hito	a man of developed *hara*	an ego-free (self-effacing) person, a tolerant (disciplined) person
Hara-no-suwatta-hito	a man of sedate *hara*	an irresolute man, a sedate man
Hara-no-kuroi-hito	a man of black *hara*	a scheming person
Hara-de-kangaeru	think with *hara*	*hara*-think (my coinage), think extra-logically, think uncalculatingly

HARA LANGUAGE	LITERAL TRANSLATION	CULTURAL TRANSLATION
Hara-no-naka-o-misenai	not showing the inside of one's *hara*	not revealing one's true motives or showing one's cards
Hara-no-saguriai	feel each other's *hara*	feel each other out, feel each other's pulse
Hara-ni-osameru	keep something in one's *hara*	keep something to oneself
Hara-ga-tatsu	*hara* stands up	get angry
Hara-mo-tatanai	even *hara* does not stand up	it's beyond indignation
Hara-ni-kiku	listen to one's *hara*	follow one's conscience
Hara-o-neru	train one's *hara*	try to gain imperturbability
Hara-no-nerete-inai-hito	a man with untrained *hara*	a shallow thinker without experience
Hara-o-kimeru	make up one's *hara*	make up one's mind once and for all
Hara-o-sueru	set one's *hara*	brace oneself, be prepared
Hara-o-waru	slit open one's *hara*	get things off one's chest
Hara-o-miseru	show one's *hara*	show sincerity
Hara-o-watte-hanasu	open one's *hara* and talk	let it all hang out, talk things over without reserve
Hara-o-yomu	read one's *hara*	read into one's mind
Itakumonai-hara-o-saguru	having one's *hara* treated when it feels no pain	be unjustly suspected
Hara-ni-ichimotsu-aru	have something in one's *hara*	have an axe to grind

33

HARA LANGUAGE	LITERAL TRANSLATION	CULTURAL TRANSLATION
Hara-ni-suekaneru	cannot put something in one's hara	cannot put up with, cannot stomach (an insult)
Hara-o-kukuru	fasten one's hara	burn one's bridges
Hara-no-mushi-ga-osamaranai	stomach worms cannot be pacified	cannot control one's feelings
Hara-no-futoi (or futtoppara-na)	having a fat hara	forgiving or tolerant

b. *Where does* hara *belong, in the East or in the West?*
Is *hara* as unique to Japan as the author claims it is? Does the basic concept of *hara* belong to the East of which Japan is a part, if it does not belong to the West? This question, which I have repeatedly asked myself, set me on an odyssey of discovery. These are some of the responses I obtained from local people I encountered during these trips:

A Greek businessman said, "A man of big *hara*? It's a guy with a middle-aged spread." A French diplomat said, "Nothing like that; the closest to it is visceral rapport. A man who possesses it is called a *Grand Seigneur*."

An American man said, "We don't call it stomach. It belongs to heart. A man of big *hara* is called a big-hearted man. Or simply he's big."

A Hawaiian Ho'oponopono cleansing practitioner: "What you call *hara* is called *mana* in the Hawaiian language, meaning divine energy, which is stored in a memory bank called Unihipili (subconscious level). It cries like a baby: "Forgive me. I forgive you. Or 'Set me free'."

If a man of *hara* is translated as a forgiving and forgetting man, a man of *mana* is close to a man willing to cleanse himself and others by deeper breathing and creating the atmosphere, as well, that surrounds them before any interaction begins such as at the negotiation table.

Hawaii is where East meets West. I turned heel and went East, visiting such countries as S. Korea, Taiwan, Singapore, Malaysia, Mainland China, Tibet (now part of China), Nepal, Thailand and India. The Chinese ideograph *hara*, probably meaning courageous equanimity, was found in the holy scripture at a Buddhist temple.

But the transmutable nature of *hara* was not to be discovered, until, that is, I visited Tibet and Nepal to learn from Tantric Buddhism the circular motion that says birth means death because every human goes through the process called wheel of existence: 1) ignorance, 2) activities (moral or immoral), 3) consciousness (rebirth), 4) mind or matter, 5) the Six Spheres of Sense, 6) contact, 7) feeling, 8) craving, 9) grasping, 10) actions (karma), 11) birth, 12) decay, death, sorrow, lamentation, pain, grief and despair.

Suffering comes full circle. Spinning the prayer wheel Tibetan monks carry with them on their pilgrimage, I discovered that things don't go straight in the East. They go circularly like the I-Ching in China or the wheel of existence in the Tibetan province of China. I went to Lumbini, in Nepal, known as the birth place of Gautama Buddha, and sat for many hours under the sal tree hoping to get inside the womb of Maya Devi, the Lord's mother, and identify with the *hara* of Buddha. Strangely, Buddha and *Kwannon* (female Buddha, but actually both are gender neutral) never fail to accept me in their stomach whenever I sit in front of either of them. The proof of the infinity of his *hara* can be found in the hanging picture scroll of his nirvana (his death or sleep?) surrounded by mourners, not only humans, friends or foes, but wild animals.

Buddha's hara embraces all forms of life in the entire ecosystem of the earth, so why not a doubting researcher like me?

I saw an Indian movie, *ARTH*, in Nepal with the hope of getting into the psyche of Indians, and found the essence of *hara* in it. It was the story of a woman who first went through traumatic periods of mental agony, became very jealous of her husband having an affair with another woman, but eventually rose above her emotional conflict to find perfect harmony with herself. The movie

35

purified my soul, because the heroine fit into my ideal image of *Kwannon* (Embodiment of Mercy), being gentle, tender-hearted, tolerant of her husband's affair, dedicated, selfless and principled (she refused to remarry). When the jealous woman stops feeling jealous and abandons her desires, everyone, her husband and his lover, kneel down before her and beg her mercy tearfully.

The moral of the story:
The one who goes up, comes down. (Anyone who wins, loses).
The one who laughs, cries.
The one who tortures others is tortured.
The one who gets, gives.

The irony of the wheel of existence exemplified in the tear-jerking Indian movie convinced me that it pays to have *hara*, and *hara*, like still water, runs deep. *Hara* is a big ocean. What is an ocean? It is a birthplace of life on earth, the planet of water. It is the amorphous nature of water that attracts people, and by the same token it is the nebulous *en* (predetermination) that brings people together.

Hara is the vital energy that radiates the web of *en* (pronounced *yuen* in Chinese). The Japanese are fond of using the word *en* (not be confused with yen, the Japanese currency) rather than referring to "coincidence," even in casual daily conversation.

"It's a strange *en* (fate) that we bumped into each other on the street again, isn't it?"

"Yes, *en* is strange."

"*En* brought me here. Because one thing leads to another, I've found myself in this business."

En like *hara* is hard to define. *En* is predetermined. *Hara* is undeterminable. And yet both go *beyond time and space*. *En* is definitely Oriental. In many Buddhist countries I visited, whenever I spoke of *en* and wrote it down in *Kanji* on paper as a means of getting instant rapport, they nodded and smiled.

How Oriental is *en*?

My curiosity led me on to the University of Sanskrit where I happened to meet a professor by the name of Prof. Tej Keshari Shrma. His impromptu talk on zero, hara and truth in Sanskrit was enlightening. He explained as follows: "Zero consists of two processes of going (*sangama*) and coming to appear (*samagama*). Zero gets to 1. 1 gets to 9 and 1 plus 0. And 1 keeps getting zeros to reach eternity—and back to zero. Zero is continuation. Zero is *en*. Zero is the truth."

I exclaimed: "Eureka!" It was an instant intellectual *satori* (enlightenment). "How do you say the *hara* in Sanskrit which I explained a little while ago?" I asked excitedly.

"Kundalini," was the professor's answer.

Serpentine kundalini is an energy source in humans. The *hara*, coiled like a snake, must be ready to spiral upward and outward. If *hara* is void (sunyatta), it must be a coiled energy form that enables the void to reappear.

Haragei is a zero game in which unconscious performers vie for continuation: zero. It takes a long *michi* (road) to travel to identify with zero.

c. Sizing up of hara

In Japan, one often hears seasoned businessmen say, "In your twenties, you must improve your mind, but in your thirties you must develop your *hara*." This, of course, does not mean one has to develop a pot belly to look more impressive or intimidating in business negotiations.

Hara, in this parlance, means big-heartedness, including caring, understanding, and tolerance for different views, gained through experience. A man of *hara*, or *harano-aru-hito*, as we say in Japan, is one who usually listens and seldom argues. A man of *hara* accepts things, people or arguments included, as they come and seldom makes value judgements or gets personally or emotionally involved. No remark, thus, is more insulting than: "He has *atama* (head) but not *hara*," because anyone who lacks *hara* is not in full control of himself.

When a popular Diet member of the ruling party, Ichiro Nakagawa, committed suicide, everyone said in lamentation, "How can a man who looks so tough do a thing like that?", "After all, he was a man of a pure heart," and "He's such a well-liked person, that's why he couldn't survive." Not a single person spoke ill of the dead politician, with the sole exception of my wife, Setsuko, who said to me in private, "After having heard all the testimony of his friends and relatives on the special TV programs on his death, I came to the conclusion: "He had a big head, a big heart, but a small *hara*. But I know that this is the last comment a Japanese (with *hara*) would dare make in public."

Hara often means *utsuwa* (vessel) or potential. "He has no *utsuwa*" means "He hasn't got what it takes to become a man of *hara*." Feeling out each other's "unproven potential" (*hara*) is the name of the game in the *haragei* country of Japan, because it is common knowledge that one's *hara* must not be analyzed but subtly felt. This is why *mondo* or "undialectic" dialogue replaces arguments. The *mondo* is circular and frustrates Westerners, as described in the novel *The Ambassador* by Morris West:

> Sometimes I walk in the garden and watch the monks tending the plants, steadily, particularly, "making of each grass blade a Golden Buddha." Sometimes I sit in the house of Muso Soseki, cross-legged on a straw mat, drinking tea which he has infused for me in ceremonial fashion and following him through that meditative method of dialogue which is called *mondo* . . .
>
> "Why do you come to this place?"
> "To seek enlightenment."
> "Why have you not found it?"
> "Because I seek it."
> "How will you find it?"
> "By not seeking."
> "Where will you find it?"
> "In no place."
> "When will you find it?"
> "At no time."

The pattern of the dialogue is like the pattern of the temple and the house and the garden. Everything is allusive, condensed, and yet infinitely extended, just as the mat on which we sit seems to flow outward through the veranda and merge with the sand of the dry garden.

Muso Soseki, a Zen monk, is, according to the novel, also a poet, gardener, and master of calligraphy and the art of printing from wood blocks. To me, he is also an educator-trainer of developed *hara* because he knows how to size up people's *hara* through *mondo*.

Failure to grasp the *hara* of the Zen monk automatically discredits you as a man of no *hara*, *hara-no-nai-hito* as we say in Japan. Some Westerners argue: "Wait a minute! You talk about men of *hara*. Why not women of *hara*?" My answer to the question: It is possible for a woman to grow up to be a woman of *hara*; but it is not probable that a woman will develop the logic of *hara* unless she really tries harder or the Japanese tradition tries harder to accommodate change. Will I be able to prove it? Let me try.

Suppose a liberated Japanese woman, a graduate of an American business school with a masters degree in business administration (MBA), knocks on the door of a Zen monk. The monk will size up her *hara* (unproven capacity), rather than her credentials or scholastic accomplishments.

"It's a great honor to see you, Mr. Tachibana."

"What can I do for you?"

"The purpose of my visit here is to seek your advice on my career choice. I want to be a professional business woman in Japan. And I wonder if there is any job opening for a Japanese woman like me. I understand you have many contacts, such as Konosuke Matsushita and other business tycoons."

". . . You are going to get married, aren't you?"

"Not for the time being, no. How many years do you think it will take before I establish myself, so to speak?"

". . . You are not going to get married for the time being. Why not?"

"Because I want to commit myself to work. I don't want to end up being just another housewife doing housework."

". . . It'll take ten years."

"Ten years? I don't understand. I'm an MBA. And I did far better than many male students in school. When it comes to problem-solving skills, I can hold my own. I have no problem communicating in English."

". . . It'll take fifteen years."

"Fifteen years?"

"You'll be getting married in the future, won't you?"

"What's that got to do with my career choice?"

". . . Have a cup of tea."

"Oh, I'm sorry. I'm so upset. To answer your question, sir, I cannot rule out the possibility of getting married."

"For that matter, you cannot rule out the possibility of having a baby, can you?"

"No. But I'll probably get my future husband to take care of it. No problem."

". . . If he says no?"

"I won't marry such a man. I can support my husband. I just want to lose myself in my business. I'm an independent woman trained in America; that's why I'm here without any letter of reference."

". . . It will take twenty years."

"Wait a second! I'm not saying all this just to satisfy my ego. You see, I have a sick mother who's been bedridden for the past five years. I have a moral obligation to support her. I'm not one of those irresponsible Japanese women you see these days. I'm driven by an old Japanese value: emotional commitment, if you will."

". . . It'll take twenty-five years."

"Twenty-five years?"

". . . You haven't drunk your tea yet."

"Never mind. I'll be fifty by then. How can a woman work as a business woman at that age? You don't understand how seriously I'm committed to becoming an influential business woman—useful for society."

". . . Useful for society? It'll take thirty years."

"I beg your pardon. You're just a monk. You don't know anything about business. You don't understand a woman's heart."

". . . With that *hara* of yours, you'll never make it in Japan."

"You never know."

". . . I know it by my *hara*. You didn't place your shoes properly at the entrance, did you?"

"How do you know?"

". . . The way you talked and the way you breathed."

The above is a grossly exaggerated case of how a mind-logical woman and *hara*-logical monk can talk at cross-purposes. The straightforward woman thought linearly that every problem has a solution, whereas the holistic monk thought non-linearly or rather circularly that the problem is the solution and conversely the solution is the problem. Worse still, the woman listened hard and responded strongly to every word expressed without hearing inaudible breaths, whereas the monk heard her breaths but barely listened to her arguments. Obviously they were not on the same "breathlength" with each other. Westerners stress the need for critical listening, whereas *hara*-logical Japanese emphasize non-critical "hearing," or listening between and beyond the lines, so to speak. The interjectory phrase, "How about tea?" during conversations could mean, "Take it easy," or more precisely, "Regulate your breath." Upshot: the woman's heart told her not to see the monk again. The monk's *hara* told him to wait until she came back again, enlightened, balanced, her breath regulated. Because he may have liked her guts, contrary to his words. Nobody knows his *hara*. Any person who loses control of his or her breath in Japan loses center and potential friends. Alas, the female MBA may have displayed a mind developed in an American business school, but has the woman gained *hara*? It is unfortunate that for lack of evidence on my part I cannot prove that it is nature rather than nurture that makes it more difficult for women to acquire *hara*. Just for the record, I am no biological determinist.

Hara, although a bit too ambiguous for the uninformed Westerner to understand easily, is what the Japanese comfortably identify with. For the Japanese, reality cannot be grasped through concepts and ideas. The reality of *hara* goes beyond the dichotomy of we and they, or subject and object, or sadism or masochism, and cannot be analyzed or comprehended by mind-logic, but can be "experienced" by *hara*-logic.

Here is another useful episode to describe the nature of *hara-kiri*, a cousin of *haragei*. Lord Toshitada Hosokawa of Kyushu asked Musashi Miyamoto, an invincible swordmaster, what the spirit of *Bushido* (the Way of Warriors) was. Musashi said, "I cannot put it into words. I'll demonstrate it for you, Lord," and called for his disciple Tetsunosuke Koga. As soon as Koga entered his room, he shouted with mock surprise, "Bad news, Koga. You have been ordered to commit *seppuku* (ritual suicide) right now." The young samurai, without batting an eyelash, said: "May I use the next room, sir?" and solemnly prepared to commit *seppuku*.

When Koga was just about to cut open his stomach with his sword, Musashi came into the room with a happy face. "Good news, Koga. The lord ordered you to stop *seppuku*." Koga, without any expression on his face, said in a low voice, "I see," and quietly left the room. The lord heaved a sigh of relief and said to Musashi, "Now I know what the integrity of *Bushido* is." If so, the three people operated on the principle of *hara*. The lord got the message through Musashi's *haragei*. *Bushido* means *hara* first and hearts and minds second. No man of *hara* would dare ask if Musashi meant what he had said or was faking.

There is no proof that this stylized *hara*-logical approach to problem-solving also works outside Japan. A devil-may-care Japanese man once put on a good front by bluffing to a rascal in China: "You can cut off my arm before you punish this poor woman." The result: his arm was cut off, the woman punished.

d. Amae *vs* hara

What argument is to Westerners, *haragei* is to Japanese. The former is verbal boxing, wherein strategy is what counts. Argument attempts to reach the truth through conflict of opinions. The *haragei* way 'stomachs' differences and avoids conflict. In contrast to logical argumentation, *haragei* may be termed extra-logical. *Haragei* can be an effective means of creating a favorable climate for reaching an agreement in principle, submerging differences, whereas debate can be an efficient means of crystalizing the differences before solving any problem.

The United States is a why-because culture. Japan is a non-why, non-because culture. The Japanese term for why is *naze* or *wake* (pronounced *wakke*). *Wake,* roughly, means two things in the Japanese lexicon: a) reason and b) situation (or circumstance). My observations tell me that in Japan, situation takes precedence over reason. What Japanese call "reason beyond reason" (*rigai no ri*) is a *haragei* practitioner's stock in trade. The very nature of this principle-free principle leads foreign observers to suspect that the Japanese have no principles.

A partial illustration of this is the fact that Western newspapers are reason-oriented, whereas Japanese papers are emotion-oriented. One example: the *Asahi Shimbun* (afternoon edition) on Feb. 13, 1978, carried an article on a murder case, with the following headlines in order of decreasing size: The first headline said: "(Boys) Determined Previous Day to Get Revenge." The second: "The Two Showed No Expression on Their Faces." The third: "They Confessed in Detail Their Motives." The fourth: "The Junior High School Murder Incident." This didn't surprise me too much. But another example did.

I was appalled to see that the biggest headline on the inside page of one of the major dailies here said in bold type: "CHILD WAS HUNGRY FOR PARENTAL LOVE," and that a much smaller headline announced: "The Child Murdered His Grandfather." If I hadn't learned English and let it unconsciously mold my logical way of thinking, I, as an average Japanese not comfortable with Western logic, might not have been annoyed by the two

43

headlines. Neither, for that matter, might I have been annoyed by the headline of the major Japanese daily on a plane crash: "No Japanese on Board."

Even more appalling is the fact that nobody that I know of has bothered to ask why the editors put their interpretation of the situation leading to a homicide in the major headline first, and the fact (murder) in the minor headline, instead of the other way around, as in first-class Western journalism.

It seems to me the city desk was trying to establish the fact that the child killer was in a *shikataganai* (uncontrollable) situation, which caused the homicide, though not justifying the act of murder *per se*. It is like saying that a child should get away with murder because he has only one parent. I heard this once myself. This is *amae* (permissiveness), or call it the pleasure principle if you like. The *amae* logic goes like this: Everyone hates crime, but though the crime is punishable, since the person hated committing the crime or says he is sorry, we should look the other way. Contrast this circular reasoning with the reality principle by which Westerners (as well as Chinese and Koreans) operate. Their logic goes straight or syllogistically to the point: major premise—crime should be punished; minor premise—a particular person committed a crime; conclusion—therefore, he should be punished. I call this three-step logic "triangular" logic, as compared with Japanese "circular" logic, which often (not always) allows criminals to get away with minor offenses with "*sumimasen*" (I'm sorry). Mr. Gerald C. Harvey, a corporate attorney at Nissho Iwai American Corporation, said to me, "When I got myself into trouble in Japan, I apologized instead of defending myself [which he could have done]. Policemen were happy. Everyone was happy. I got away free. And *sumimasen* worked." The Japanese may deserve credit for the display of their *hara* involved in looking the other way.

Is *hara* to blame for permissiveness? No. *Hara*, though mistakenly construed as purely the seat of *amae* (permissiveness), is also the seat of non-permissiveness. For a man of *hara* within a company is not necessarily the one who readily "forgives and forgets" his men's mistakes when they feel sorry, but may be the one who refuses to be lenient. He might say angrily: "You can't get away with that by saying you're sorry." Thus the two statements, "Say you're sorry. Then you can go free," do not contradict each other. The truth is somewhere in between—the situation and not the principle. The reader can easily give the situational *amae* or *hara* (tolerance) a bad name for the excessive permissiveness in Japanese society today, in which the society has given too much *amae* (*amayakasu*) to the child who demands too much *amae* (*amaeru*) from it. *Hara* is *amae* anchored in the center.

Where does *amae* leave off and *hara* begin? Let me explain. The Japanese prelogic of *amae* (the drive to dependence—not dependence per se) goes like this: Having one parent is "*kawaiso*" or pathetic (justifying dependence). The *kawaiso* child was probably in a *shikataganai* (uncontrollable) situation (deserving sympathy). Therefore, give him *amae* by punishing his crime for him and not him for his crime. *Amae* does not punish but *hara* does. *Hara* reasons circularly: to let a bad guy get away with crime means to let crime get away with a bad guy. So it pays not to let him get away with it if the situation so dictates. Both *amae* and *hara* are circular, and never proceed straight ahead.

Consider the extraordinary case of Kenshin Uesugi, who sent desperately-needed salt to the camp of his sworn enemy, Shingen Takeda, knowing that this was tantamount to giving ammunition to an enemy firing line? It was a seemingly foolish act. War is mass murder. Murder and humanitarianism contradict each other.

This logical reasoning seems to have little validity in Japan, in view of the fact that many Japanese still give Uesugi so much credit for showing his *hara* (benevolence, courage, empathy, and caring all combined). If *amae* is inwardly negative or passive, *hara* is definitely outwardly positive and expansive. If *amae* is viewed from without as a guiding principle in Japan, the Japanese are undoubtedly miniaturizers, as Professor Lee o-Young of Seoul's Ewha Women's University argues, but if *hara* is perceived from within as the center and *amae* the periphery, the Japanese are both shrinkers and stretchers. If *amae* is human nature, *hara* is nature in humans. *Amae* could be homicidal or suicidal depending on the situation and is thus treacherous; *hara* is loyal. *Amae* is an urge to draw closer to friends; *hara* is a drive to draw closer even to enemies. *Amae* is an undisciplined desire to take the other person's *amae*·for granted, *hara* disciplines *amae's* emotions. *Amae* is at the periphery; *hara* is at the center. *Amae* is a desire for dependence; *hara* is a drive for interdependence. *Amae* is feminine; *hara* is masculine. While a man of *amae* is considered too feminine to do *haragei*, a man of *hara* qualifies for masculine *haragei* action.

The managers of predominantly male Japanese corporations are expected to have *hara* with which to deal with and "educate" their employees. *Hara* is toughness plus paternal love; *Amae* is softness minus parental discipline. It took the *hara* of Soichiro Honda, founder of internationally competitive Honda Motors, to get his company to where it is now.

This macho founder had to make some painful decisions along the way, including the dismissal of his own brother from management, and the transformation of the corporate name. Honda employees admired their "Godfather's" *hara*-based decision but refused to accept the corporate name change lest it destroy the well-established corporate identity. It takes an *oyabun* (paternal boss) like Honda-*san* to turn his own company around. The more cellular and cohesive the family business is, the more *hara*-discipline and "*oyabun*manship" (The Art of Management in Japan) is required in people management decision-making, especially where expansion and growth are the chief targets. *Amae* guarantees and encourages individual security; *Hara* gets rid of the security blanket and promotes group discipline without sacrificing individual security.

Based on the assumption that people are the greatest risk of all risks in corporate family business management, the top executives of the successful corporations in Japan are expected to possess and demonstrate *hara*: being by nature tough with insiders and soft with outsiders. It's even tougher to be an employee related by blood to the corporate executives of the masculine family concerns.

A war, or a serious game, must be played to win, not to lose. So each is likely to develop into a science rather than an art. But in Japan, wars must be fought "aesthetically" so as not to allow the winner to "over-win," or the loser to "over-lose." Since war is likely to develop into an art, rather than a science, there is room for *amae* and *hara*. It's not whether one wins or loses (a game); but how aesthetically one wins or loses (an art). It's a *haragei* solution. It is no wonder *haragei* performers are intent on winning the *hara* as well as the hearts and minds of the third party (watchers) lest any single person playing the circular game should lose face.

Interestingly, however, in the West a war of words on a different plane is inevitable: Grantland Rice, the famous sportswriter, argues, "It's not whether you win or lose, but how you play the game." Vince Lombardi, the equally famous football coach, argues back, "Winning isn't everything; it's the only thing." The conflict of opinions is amusing to the Japanese, who grew up hearing people say, "To lose is to win." This is an old *amae* tactic of eventually getting one up on enemies by playing a why-is-everyone-picking-on-poor-little-me game. The Japanese favorite practice of bargaining from the position of weakness or crying wolf is also an applied science of *amae*. Both tactics lack *hara*, since users expect others to show *hara* without showing their own *hara*.

Be that as it may, it remains true that in the West games must be played between at least two "independent" parties. Logic tells us both can't be winners and losers of the game at the same time. An individual can expect to win or lose. But *haragei*, not inherently a zero-sum game, must be "interdependently" performed by more than one actor who considers it a shame to show *amae*, or to expect favorable feedback from the audience. Whether or not the audience "feels" *hara* in actors is the key to the success of *haragei* performance, or of any theatrical art for that matter. Too little *hara* or too much *amae* can spoil *haragei*.

2. *Gei* (Art)

Haragei means the *gei* (art) of *hara*. The practitioners of *haragei* are therefore artists, not players. *Haragei* can be a highly polished theatrical art performed off stage. But it takes real-life connoisseurs to really appreciate it. The art is in *not* showing one's true intent but in hiding it; it must be subtly and effortlessly performed to be appreciated only by those who really appreciate it. It is not art for the masses; it is private art for the intimate. In all traditional Japanese arts there are the same underlying characteristics that discipline the real-life artists while enabling a natural flow of self-expression: *ishin-denshin, ma,* and *michi* (the Way).

a. Ishin-denshin

To transcend the conflict between objectivity and subjectivity, Eastern mysticism is based on direct insights, rather than on logical interpretations. Seeing a thing and being a part of it is the basis of knowing and understanding. Zen painting is an art of *ishin-denshin* (heart-to-heart understanding); that is, an intuitive art. The Zen master experiences the object and lets the object draw the picture through the ink brush.

To use a phrase by Zeami, what is vital for Noh artists is *riken-no-ken,* which means to see oneself dancing through the eyes and mind of the audience. The *haiku,* a classical Japanese verse of just seventeen syllables, also seems to be an outgrowth of this concept. A *haiku* demands that its readers also read themselves, and thus become more aware and a part of what the *haiku* attempts to say. *Ishin-denshin* is a quintessential part of *haragei* communication, in which what one feels must be what others feel.

Ishin-denshin can cut both ways. Take a touch-and-go situation involving an artist (the tea master) and his patron (a shogun), for instance. Too intimate a knowledge of each other's ulterior motives (e.g. ambition) may help preserve *ishin-denshin* on one hand but could prove to be hazardous on another if the balance of each other's *hara* breaks.

Since the artist-patron relationship is fragile, it takes a subtle display of *hara* as a ballast to maintain the otherwise lopsided relationship.

Without it, too much reliance upon *ishin-denshin* can result in a catastrophe. A case in point is the historic conflict of *hara* between Shogun Hideyoshi (1536–1593), enamored of the tea ceremony, and a great tea master, Sen-no-Rikyu (1521–1591), a founder of *Cha-no-yu* (the tea cult). Opinions and speculation are varied among scholars and critics as to the exact reason why Hideyoshi ordered Rikyu, whom he so highly respected as his tea master, to commit a ceremonial *hara-kiri* suicide. Here are some of the legitimate reasons:

First, *intellectual*. Because the two representative leaders of respective worlds, politics and art, could not see eye to eye on the esoteric principle of the ritual at a tea ceremony.

Second, *personal*. Because Rikyu refused to offer his daughter to Hideyoshi as his concubine when requested, he caused his lord to lose face.

Third, *emotional*. Because Rikyu objected to Hideyoshi's decision to go on a Korean expedition. Rikyu is reported to have made a slip of the tongue when he said, "Fighting Koreans is not so easy as fighting Mitsuhide Akechi [a traitor who killed Nobunaga, Hideyoshi's master]."

Fourth, *political*. Because Rikyu, immediately after his lord's return from his Korean expedition, unwisely colluded with the wrong group, which argued for decentralization of power, instead of the group which believed in centralization. There is another political reason why Rikyu was ordered to commit *harakiri*. Rumor says that an anti-Rikyu faction grew beyond the control of the Shogun.

Fifth, *ethical*. Because Rikyu infuriated Hideyoshi in two ways: one, Rikyu ordered his men, without prior consultation with Hideyoshi, to place his wooden figure on the *Kin-mo-kaku* in front of the Daitoku Temple; two, Rikyu made a windfall profit out of the commercial transaction of expensive tea utensils. In other words, Rikyu overstepped his *bun* (bound) as an artist.

Sixth, *psychological*. Because Hideyoshi, ranking higher than Rikyu, had reason to feel bitter about Rikyu's occasional slips of the tongue on matters related to politics. This justifies the theory that Rikyu lost a power game. To make matters worse, Hideyoshi knew all along that Rikyu was one of the *nouveau riche*, from the low status of a merchant family, while Rikyu knew too much about his lord's background, like the fact that Hideyoshi, born into a poor peasant family, was an upstart. To be too intimate about each other's weaknesses meant that something had to give. In other words, both knew too much about each other to remain on the same breathlength. *Ishin-denshin* worked negatively.

b. Ma

Ma, the second characteristic of art, means space, room, an interval, or a pregnant pause. *Ma* is that moment unbridled by contradictions—contrasts between part and whole; it is the moment that allows one to be aware of and part of his surroundings. As Dr. Edward T. Hall explains: "When Westerners think and talk about space, they mean the distance between objects. In the West we are taught to perceive and to react to the arrangements of objects and to think of space as empty. The meaning of this becomes clear only when it is contrasted with the Japanese who are trained to give meaning to spaces, to perceive the shape and arrangement of spaces—for this they have a word, *ma*. The *ma*, or interval, is a basic building block in all Japanese spatial experience." (*The Hidden Dimension*, Anchor, page 153)

One example which Dr. Hall cites of this abstract concept is the fifteenth-century Zen monastery garden of Ryoanji in Kyoto, famous for the beauty of its dry garden with nothing but rocks and gravel arranged asymmetrically. Upon first glance at what Prof. Alexander Alland, Jr., professor of cultural anthropology, calls a garden of absences, the unreceptive mind may find little worthy of contemplation. But with patience one begins to identify with *ma* in motion and space.

Zen masters, who are by definition masters of *ma*, consider the garden to be poetry, philosophy, landscaping, and symbolic art, or all of them put together. As one "experiences" the *ma* instead of "analyzing" it, one develops rapprochement with nature through *ma* experience. By yielding to the extra-dimensional *ma*, even music can be heard.

Zeami, the founding genius of the Noh theater in the four-teenth century, wrote, "The feeling of concentrated intensity in the depths of the actor's heart is sensed by the audience and thus the silent pauses are made interesting." *Ma* suggests things unspoken—gestures that are effortless. It is that aspect of art which implies but doesn't confirm. But it goes without saying that there must be no evidence of effort and it takes many years of constant training to reach this level of meaningful non-perform-ing.

I am reminded of an occasion when I accompanied a particu-larly intelligent Jewish labor leader of the AFL-CIO. He was one of the most articulate lecturers I had ever interpreted for. The man, proud of having been a good orator in the United States, asked me why there was no feedback from the Japanese audi-ence. At a loss to explain in detail the meaning of *ma* in English, I answered, in an overly-simplified manner: "Because you were articulate." My comment was obviously inadequate. For what I meant was this: "Your speech was so neatly organized that the Japanese audience, deprived of *ma*, didn't know how to identify with you non-verbally, much less to relate to you verbally."

It seems to me that Western conversationalists listen to the words between pauses, whereas Japanese *haragei* practitioners listen more attentively to the pauses between the words and gestures. One doesn't need the art of persuasion that underlies Western communication practices to be a successful communica-tor in Japanese society. In fact, *haragei* performers are verbally inadequate in front of others, and by no means logical, coherent, or articulate, because they give *ma* full play. It is not surprising to learn then that the top salesmen of stocks, bonds, or insurance often turn out not to be smooth or slick talkers.

There is in Japan no historical evidence of great public orators like those known in the West. It is not surprising, by the same token, that great public speakers or articulate persuaders are vir-tually non-existent among top executives in Japanese corpora-tions. With the Japanese tendency to give full play, as Professor Richard Pascale, author of *The Art of Japanese Management*, says, to *ma* (or what Prof. Frederick Massarich of UCLA calls "functional ambiguity"), it would not be surprising if *ma*-less employees spun out of the center of gravity within the circular corporate structure.

The master of *haragei* invariably understands *ma* and exercises it unconsciously. Evidence says a man of *hara* is more likely to finish first at the center of corporate gravity. Men of smaller *hara*, with less luck, usually end up at the periphery in a race to get to the inner core of the corporate family. Therefore, a chief executive officer must be capable, as a central figure, of exerting both centrifugal (moving outward away from a center) and centripetal (moving inward toward an axis) powers to keep the family circular.

I recall as a one-time executive assistant at Nikko Securities Co., Ltd. hearing a chief executive officer murmuring in the executive elevator, "The toughest job for a president of a company is to make the sole decision on the demotion and spinning off of directors to lower ranks or subsidiaries en masse. And it's really bad for the system." The president of a "parent" company (*oyagaisha*), being always in the center of the corporate group, surrounded by its "children" companies (*kogaisha*) or subsidiaries like the pivotal sun in the solar system, must be very sensitive in putting its redundant directors out to yet another pasture—away from the center of gravity. Without *hara* he gets an ulcer; with *hara* as a security blanket he gets by.

According to Teruo Goko, in the Japanese language there are two kinds of "things": *mono* and *koto*. The former refers to properties, or matter and energy, while the latter refers to organizing relationships, or information, that connect various *mono*, thus producing a certain object or logical system, or what is called *kotogara* in Japanese. At the same time, the Japanese language has two more concepts—*ma* and *aida*—which represent coordinates. Thus *ma* is a place or a local area in the coordinate space where a *mono* lies, while *aida* is a relation that connects different *ma* to produce *aidagara*, which can best be translated as "context." In my terminology, this is the very form of a physical system with the resultant conclusion that the Japanese are contextualists.

All this illustrates that the Japanese tendency to identify with an undefinable *ma*, or context, is likely to find a niche in corporate communication where the dividing line between management and labor is blurred.

Konosuke Matsushita, chairman of the board of the giant Matsushita group, surprised many a foreign correspondent when he said publicly, "I'm not afraid of aggressive labor movements. I might even work as a union leader for them." Although he was referring to his own close-knit company's union, the unspoken message of the management lord was clear: management and labor are one at Matsushita.

Konosuke Matsushita, proven master of *ma* in people-management, seldom orders, but when he says something, everyone listens. Nobody around him is insensitive enough to ask him if his remark is a mere suggestion or an order. As it turns out, everyone is made to feel at the gut level that they are the initiators . . . the bosses. Each Matsushita man, or employee of other successful corporations in Japan for that matter, is made to feel part employee and part employer. The rationale behind this is that the management of people is art, while the management of figures is science. Worker satisfaction, loyalty, and motivation come from workers themselves, not from above or from the system, because man by nature is in conflict between the desire to lead and to be led. The success story of Matsushita results from the successful employment of *ma* in corporate communication including industrial relations.

Since the time of Plato most scholars have believed that the mind and body are of a different nature. Western anatomy is concerned with the human organism as a structure which can be taken apart like pieces of machinery to determine how the parts fit together to work. The mind influences the body and dominates over it. The mind is considered superior to the body and the spirit superior to both the body and the mind. Superiority of the mind is overly emphasized in business schools in the U.S.A. Prof. Pascale, author of *The Art of Japanese Management*, observes: "American managers tend to overfocus on the "hard" elements." Some of the best work done in business schools in recent decades has been in advancing our understanding of the "cold triangle" of strategy, structure, and systems. Each one and the relationships among the three are particularly susceptible to analytical, quantitative, logical, and systematic investigation. In short, "science" of one kind or another, rigorous observation, and conceptualization—*thinking*, if you prefer—were required.

The triangle, because of lack of *ma*, means tension or aloofness to circular-minded Japanese. A Western sense of individuality arises from a "linear" awareness: the believer must establish a linear or triangular rather than circular relationship with God. Japanese insist that God, nature, and man are one and the same, embracing a flowing rather than fixed, definitive form of religion—by no means triangular. To the Japanese, an individual life is an interrelationship of body, mind, and spirit: the circle. The Japanese mentality is the mandala (meaning circle), representing the cosmos or the potent core of psychic energy. It is a balance of force whose beginning is in its end, whose end is in its beginning: the circle. From this one can assume that *hara*-logic may have had its origin in tantric Buddhism.

Origins aside, in a tension-filled triangular-shaped American company, employees try hard to get ahead of one another in a race to make it to the top, while in circular-shaped Japanese companies, where one-upmanship or gamesmanship is frowned upon for aesthetic reasons, employees are encouraged not to steal a march on others in a race to close in on the axis (the center of *wa*) lest they end up being spun off.

In the American corporate environment, competition is the name of the game, whereas in the Japanese, disciplined competition is. The Japanese notion of *wa* is the *ma* between competition and cooperation. The reason why Tokugawa Ieyasu, the longest-ruling *wa*-preserving shogun in the history of Japan, is so widely read and emulated by corporate executives in Japan, is that he proved himself a great user (to some a manipulator) of his men and the wisdom of *ma* . One of his adroit methods of keeping people under his control was the well-known balancing act of keeping "insider" (*fudai*) *daimyos* worse-paid and "outside" (*tozama*) *daimyos* better-paid, thus keeping his sphere of power harmoniously circular.

c. Michi *(Way)*

The Japanese word *michi* means two things: first, roads, ways, or alternatives; second, the Way (singular). The Way is the spiritual foundation on which ways must be built. The word is also pronounced *do*, when attached as a suffix to any cultural pursuit such as *kado* (flower arrangement), *chado* (tea ceremony), or martial arts, such as *judo, kendo,* or *karatedo. Chado* (or *sado*) is not just the art (*jutsu*) of making or serving tea; it is a way of life (*michi*), since it involves spiritual commitment on a full-time basis. By this line of reasoning, it was not surprising that I came up with *eigodo,* English-learning as a way of life and art. When people ask me what *eigodo* means, I answer: "Learning English through *hara.*"

The wisdom of *eigodo* came partly from a casual conversation with Mr. Nanrei Ozeki, my mentor and a Zen monk at the Ryokoin Temple in Kyoto, who inspired me to combine English-learning and Zen.

When I was first led to his tea-room, I immediately sputtered out my theory of *eigodo* to grab his attention.

"Don't you think there is *kokoro* in learning English?"

The monk remained silent. So I carried on.

"There is ugliness in beauty and beauty in ugliness."

"*Sorede*? (And then?)"

"Therefore, there is *kokoro* in English."

"*Sorede*?"

"I mean, believing mind is not two and non-two mind is believing mind. That's what Zen is all about, isn't it? Sir?"

"*Sorede*?"

My breathing got shallower and shallower, and I felt uneasy. But I tried to pull myself together and kept on talking.

"The *kokoro* of an individual determines everything."

"*Soredake*? (Nothing more?)" the monk said.

"I mean, my mind tells me what I think. It is the 'I.'"

"What is the 'I' then? If you cut off your finger, it's no longer yours, is it?"

Taken aback by this unexpected question, I was speechless.

"Your theory is correct but your foundation is shaky. Zen is not as complicated as you think. I served you tea a little while ago. But you didn't drink it. When you are carried away by something, you miss everything else. You didn't hear the chirping of birds outside. How can you appreciate the beauty that surrounds you when you can't even enjoy the taste of the tea I served you? *Kokoro* is everywhere. Even in learning a foreign language."

"I see." I was frozen into silence.

The monk continued with his eyes glaring at me. I trembled and listened in silence. Toning down his voice, he said,

"Let me demonstrate to you what a martial art is. Push this fire tong in front of you. . . . And pull it. I didn't resist anything, did I? This is what *kendo* (the art of swordmanship) is all about."

Awed by the quiet and yet intense presence of the monk, I was like a little frog at the sight of a huge snake. I cried in the train on my way home, telling myself, "I lost completely."

And the tears of joy started to roll down my cheeks.

The monk was hardly polite, but he *hara*-talked me into a *satori* that the *michi* of *eigo* (English learning) is not in one's mind but in one's *hara*.

The notion of *michi*, being the beginningless beginning and the endless ending, is circular. The philosophy behind world-famous Morita psychotherapy, being harmonization of one's actions with the phenomenal world, might be *michi*-seeking in the sense that it emphasizes rapprochement with nature. Since Morita philosophy is close to a modernized version of Zen, David Reynolds, an American anthropologist, says it is "more than" a technique (*jutsu*) for healing, judging from the fact that Morita therapy does not cure patients, but helps them to be able to cope once again. It may call for technique to cure patients, but strictly speaking it takes *gei* (subtler than art) to make patients feel that they have "made it," not that they have been "cured" by professionals.

Hara must be developed. *Gei* must be polished. Improvement of both may entail lifelong commitment; therefore, art is the Way. From this, a conclusion may be drawn: *haragei* has a Way of its own or a long road toward its perfection: selflessness.

The highest form of *haragei* is non-action. "Non-action does not mean doing nothing and keeping silent," says the Chinese philosopher Chuang-tsu. "Let everything be allowed to do what it naturally does, so that its nature will be satisfied."

To continue onward with *michi* is to allow the creative spirit to arise naturally from us, from the *hara*. Eugen Herrigel claims in his book, *Zen in the Art of Archery*, that it took him many years of practice to learn to draw the bow spiritually, with a kind of effortless strength, and to release the string without intention, letting the shot fall from the bow like a ripe fruit (*The Tao of Physics*, page 112).

To attain this stage of effortlessness in life is not easy. One's life consists of four seasons: spring, summer, autumn, and winter, each having a characteristic feature (neither positive nor negative) of its own. It is tacitly understood that *haragei* is more effortlessly performed by people beyond their autumn (from 40 through 60 years, by my count) or in their winter (60 and over) stages of development because they have seemingly come a long way in acquiring *hara* through the ups and downs and twists and turns in life. Yet it does not follow that no one in the summer stage can perform *haragei*, nor that all those advanced in age can perform *haragei*. Any person who has not gone through critical passages in life has a long *michi* (road) to travel before reaching the age where *haragei* is artlessly and effortlessly performed.

The kind of man Japanese admire for selflessness is Toshio Doko, in his late eighties these days, former Keidanren leader, now desperately promoting administrative reform. He is driven by something beyond his ego, unlike self-actualized Western executives who have made it in office: a corner office with two windows, a company jet, a secretary willing to work extra hours, keys to the executive washroom, and other coveted perks. Doko, living in a shabby house, eats coarse meals, wears old shoes, and desires virtually nothing except to actualize his altruistic motive: administrative reform. He is driven by his *hara* or nature.

Michi, says Edward G. Seidensticker, has been at the center of things, one of the supporting pillars, for a long time. If *michi* or *do* is a guiding principle, as indeed it is for many Japanese although rarely avowed, then it is almost a religion. Who can say Japanese have no principles, just because they have no system of religious belief? *Michi* shadows every art form. Zen offers an intuitive link between art and *michi*.

The following excerpt from *Zen and Japanese Culture* by Dr. Daisetsu Suzuki illustrates brilliantly how even the skills of burglary can be developed by the master of burglary who has supposedly attained *michi* (perfection or truth) in burglary art.

If people ask me what Zen is like, I say that it is like learning the art of burglary. The son of a burglar saw his father growing older and thought, "If he is unable to carry on his profession, who will be the breadwinner of the family, except myself? I must learn the trade." He suggested the idea to his father, who approved of it.

One night the father took the son to a big house, broke through the fence, entered the house, and, opening one of the large chests, told the son to get in and pick out the clothing. As soon as the son got into it, the father dropped the lid and securely applied the lock. The father now came out to the courtyard and loudly knocked at the door, waking up the whole family; then he quietly slipped away through the hole in the fence. Ther residents got excited and lighted candles, but they found that the burglar had already gone. The son, who was still securely confined in the chest, thought of his cruel father. He was greatly mortified, then a fine idea flashed upon him. He made a noise like the gnawing of a rat. The family told the maid to take a candle and examine the chest. When the chest was unlocked, out came the prisoner, who blew out the light, pushed away the maid, and fled. The people ran after him. Noticing a well by the road, he picked up a large stone and threw it into the water. The pursuers all gathered around the well trying to find the burglar drowning himself in the dark hole.

In the meantime he went safely back to his father's house. He blamed his father angrily for his narrow escape. Said the father, "Be not offended, my son. Just tell me how you got out of it." When the son told him all about his adventures, the father remarked, "There you are. You have learned the art."

This is how one should learn the art; not be taught step by step by others. This is, by the same token, how one should learn to do business, not be taught systematically by superiors. The acquisition of skills in art or in human interaction should be grasped intuitively by experience. The true leader of *hara* does not believe in teaching a lesson but giving experience in a manner exemplified in the above excerpt and also by the earlier example of Matsushita's artful people-management.

Hara is difficult to develop through intellectual processes like reading books or hearing lectures, but relatively easy when given the infusion of experience. *Hara*, for most people, like wine, improves with age.

The life of an average man or woman goes through three stages of *hara* development:

1) *Child*: hara-free stage. Children cannot control emotions, feelings, or compulsion. They "tell it like it is," compulsively. This shows that they lack *hara*. Children learn to play games—telling it like it isn't.

2) *Adult*: hara-developing stage. Situational ethics. People learn to practice emotional control—the first step in mastering *haragei*. They learn the art of *gaman* (it takes *hara* to be patient), and discipline themselves not to ask why. They play games, but cannot perform *haragei* yet.

3) *Parent*: hara-developed stage. They can be held account-

able for what their *hara* leads them to do. The mind can
be changed; but *hara* must be preserved, private and firm.
For a man of *hara*, his *hara* is his bond.

A man of firm *hara*, if occasion so demands, may have to stand
on his *suji* principles (to be explained later) by accepting *hara-kiri*
even for a "*shitsugen*" (a slip of the tongue) in public. It takes an old-
fashioned Japanese male to come out and say that the ultimate
form of *haragei* is *hara-kiri*.

d. Hara *Development*

It was explained a little while ago that the metaphysical *hara*
develops through three stages: Child, Adult, and Parent. However, the mere mention of the spiritual growth of *hara* as divorced
from the physical *hara* (stomach), would not be doing justice to
the psychosomatic development of *hara*, since spirit (invisible)
and matter (visible) are not separable but closely linked within the
realm of *hara*. And *hara* is the seat of body and soul.

Hence, my argument: physical exercise of your *hara* (abdomen)
should help expedite the spiritual growth of your (metaphysical)
hara and vice versa.

Zazen, sitting in a lotus position for non-thinking, definitely
helps in developing one's *hara*, or built-in nature, because it helps
negate one's human-self in favor of nature-self. *Zazen* emphasizes
correct breathing while concentrating on the solar plexus, a center
of one's *hara*. Zen monks claim, and I agree, that correct breathing
gives rise to correct thinking.

My experience of doing *zazen* tells me that the essence of Zen
teachings is, "In with nature. Out with self." Thoughts vacated
keep coming back in full circle. *Hara* grows in the process. *Hara*
developed through *zazen* experiences brings about the ultimate
harmony between nature in man and man in nature.

But *zazen* alone does not guarantee the attainment of *satori*
(awakening). *Satori* must be obtained the hard way. *Koan*, verbal
Zen exercises, accelerate the maturation process of becoming
aware of the limitations of one's logic and the potency of nature-

logic. *Koan* is a non-dialectic exercise in *hara* thinking, and its purpose is by no means a Zen puzzle, as Westerners call it, aimed at trapping the trainees into accepting the limitations of logical thinking; rather it helps truth seekers to come up with *hara*-logical answers, unfettered by a traditional true or false dichotomy—a product of mind-logic.

If *hara*-logic is nature-logic, another method of developing one's *hara* is fasting—a natural way. According to my theory of *hara*, an empty stomach means a full stomach. To put this theory of the law of nature into practice, I conducted a one-week fast (consuming only water) by myself at a spacious Zen temple on Mt. Takao near Tokyo. The lessons I learned from my fasting experience for a week included:

1. A complete turnaround in philosophy. Before, I used to think I was living by myself. After, I realized that I had been "lived" by others and by nature, and I thanked everybody and everything.
2. My *hara* expanded. On people: Before, I wanted to see people I liked. After, I wanted to see just about anybody, friendly or unfriendly. On ideas: Before, I accepted the ideas I liked. After, I became more openminded about hitherto-alien ideas.

The above evidence proves that the emptier your *hara* gets, the more tolerant you become of ideas or people regardless of your personal taste or likings. Of course, you do not have to have an empty stomach to expand your *hara*. The innate hunger for something spiritual or meaningful may make your frustration work for you in terms of *hara* development. My personal experience may further exemplify the point.

Some ten years ago, unlike E. Erikson who chose to be different in spite of his stepfather's expectation that he would become a doctor, I was too dependent on socially enforced expectations to seek the meaning of life. I was afraid this would be at the expense of my old identity as a member of a corporate family. But the identity that I thought I had established was not an individual identity, the sort Westerners refer to, but a group identity.

My identity at that time was: first, an employee; second, a member of the foreign exchange section of the big trading company Nissho-Iwai; third, Michihiro Matsumoto. I grew up a company man, kidding myself into believing that every city banker and credit company executive would bow their heads out of friendship to me. I was wrong. They saluted the corporate flag (Nissho-Iwai), and not the soldiers carrying it. What was my genuine identity? That thought had never really occurred to me.

My genuine identity crisis, if I can be allowed to call it that, emerged at the time of the merger between two major trading companies, Nissho and Iwai, when I began to have second thoughts about the coziness of my dual identity: "Identification with my former company Iwai or a newly born company Nissho-Iwai?" Many colleagues of mine (mostly Iwai men) deserted the new company, possibly for lack of emotional identification, which every loyal employee had felt for the former company. Frustration finally got the better of me and I went the way of a *ronin* (masterless *samurai*). Before I left the corporate family, my immediate boss tried to make me change my mind, saying, "Are you out of your mind? You will no longer be entitled to lifetime employment, the seniority system, or other fringe benefits. And worst of all, you'll be nothing. Think twice."

But my *hara* was made up. I quit the company to start from nothing. I thought I was a *samurai*, but everyone else thought I was a Bohemian. It was around this time, I think with hindsight, that my identity crisis reached an apex of intensity, comparable, perhaps to the one Erikson might have reached when he chose to be different. He chose the occupational identity of "artist" by trying to be different, whereas I chose to live an artist's life by identifying with nature. I left my pregnant wife and my son so I could "evaporate" (*johatsu*) somewhere to graduate from my old identity. The one month I spent soul-searching in a mountain hideout in Nagano Prefecture, away from "public eyes," was paradise for me, because I eventually "entered" myself through the *ma* (breathing spell) in my life. And I found "Gauguin" in myself.

To borrow the words of Castaneda, I successfully entered the conceptual order, which is more than a collection of opinions or facts, rather it is the basis for recognizing 'opinion' or 'fact.' My mind shrank; but my *hara* expanded. When something strange came over me, I found myself composing a poem which I had never dreamed of in my life. The poem I read in my *hara* is as follows:

> Silkworms and I,
> I and silkworms.
> Silkworms eat mulberry leaves untroubled,
> I read books troubled.
> Silkworms are strong,
> I am weak.
> Silkworms shed their skins four times throughout their life,
> Why can't I?

The emotional experience I had in "communicating" with silkworms and nature is condensed in the above poem. I doubt if I could express now the intensity of emotions I felt at that time. Through this experience of "nonordinary reality," I developed *hara*. The joy I had of having found the absolute truth in my *hara* was indescribable. While watching silkworms in the farmer's cottage grow by shedding their skins, I came to instant *satori*. The dictionary definition of the truth, being "agreement with that which is represented, correspondence to reality," is not really the truth my *hara* had long sought. It was separate reality: *hara*.

II

WHY DOES *HARAGEI* WORK IN JAPAN?

A. *Honne* vs *tatemae*—private vs public

Perhaps one of the most untranslatable Japanese words is *ura*. The word *ura* (literally, rear) is the opposite of *omote* or front. They are not contradictory but complementary. The words *ura-o-yomu* (read the rear of what is written or spoken) are not quite the same as "reading between the lines" or "reading beyond the lines," because reading the rear presupposes that the revealed *omote* is just the tip of an iceberg with the hidden *ura* demanding equal attention.

An oft-used remark, "*Hito-no-kokoro-no-ura-o-yome*" (Read the rear of another's mind), does not necessarily mean that one should be suspicious of the motives or integrity of others; it often means that one should be sensitive and caring enough to read into their unspoken desires or willingness to help.

Businessmen in Osaka say: "It's easy to read the rear of another's mind. But it isn't easy to read the rear of the rear. You've got to practice it. That's what it takes to perform *haragei*." The rear of the rear should be the front, since it comes full circle. The inference can be made from this that both *omote* and *ura* are just phenomena of circular *hara* and *hara* reveals itself both in *tatemae* (*omote* mind) and in *honne* (*ura* mind).

Westerners, not knowing that both *tatemae* and *honne* are part of the circle, are likely to conclude linearly that one of the two is true and the other false. I have heard many Westerners complain: "I can't understand the Japanese when they say, 'Yes, I agree, but . . .'" The Japanese yes-but syndrome that bothers Westerners is nothing but the two sides (visible and invisible) of an iceberg called *hara*: *tatemae* and *honne*.

The immediate reaction on the part of confused Americans might be, "Uh huh, we have public self and private self." These are two sides of a coin, rarely reversing themselves, whereas *honne* and *tatemae*, being part of the periphery of a coin, can readily overlap and reverse themselves. The Japanese mind, like traditional Japanese houses that have an *"engawa"* (verandah) serving as *"ma"* between the living rooms and the garden, has no clear demarcation line between "inside" (*honne*) and "outside" (*tatemae*). A situational use of *honne* for insiders (*uchiwa*) and *tatemae* for outsiders (*sotomono*), although it may occasionally appear outrageous to Westerners, is a commonly accepted practice in Japan. Foreigners are treated politely with only *tatemae* (outer truth) as *"gaijin"* (outsiders), and are rarely told the *honne* (inner truth), to their frustration.

A popular Catholic novelist, Shusaku Endo, well known for the unique theory he expounded that Jesus Christ should be mother rather than father to synchronize with the Japanese culture, gave a dangerously self-revealing account of his *hara* (private self) in his book *Watashi no Iyesu*. In answer to a priest's question: "Do you believe in Jesus Christ?" he answered, "Yes," because the other children had said "yes" in chorus in order to be baptized. Other quotations from the same book include: "Having doubts about the existence of God, I believe, does not mean having wrong attitudes as a Christian. That's what faith is all about, because faith means 99% doubt and 1% hope." "Faith also means dying while saying, 'I don't want to die.'" "I was forced to be baptized as a child. So, deep in my mind, I felt very uncomfortable with this type of religion [Christianity]." "I admit that I've been a Christian for a long time. But, honestly, I have not been inspired by the Bible or felt that this is something I should believe in. But I didn't quit

Christianity for two reasons. One, there were no other clothes to put on. My mother gave me these old clothes [Christianity]. Two, how can I do such an inhuman thing as taking off the clothes my beloved mother used to wear?"

The above quotations were roughly translated by myself. Though very honest, this Catholic writer makes one wonder if he is a Buddhist or a Catholic. To me he is a *tatemae* Christian, and a *honne* Buddhist. But the fact remains that many admirers of Shusaku Endo in Japan have found "human warmth" in him because he "cuts open his *hara*" (*hara-o-waru*), exposing his "private self" candidly.

Internationalization of Japanese corporations often means building more plants overseas or training employees in foreign languages and sending them overseas, contributing to the companies' increased profit and prestige overseas; rarely does it mean hiring more non-Japanese employees ("blue-eyed" outside directors) or foreign lawyers. The more they talk about "internationalization" (*kokusaika*) in *tatemae*, the harder they will have to try to keep under their hat their *honne* (nationalization).

Honne and *tatemae* must be balanced. *Tatemae*-oriented people are too aloof and distant and *mizukusai* (treating insiders as if they were outsiders), but *honne*-oriented people are too chummy with others and are likely to be looked upon with suspicion even when they have no ulterior motives. To most Japanese, foreign missionaries would be "*mizukusai*" (distant) for they give only *tatemae*.

As a college student, I vividly remember being argued down by an American missionary of Christianity with Bible (*tatemae*) punches. The round of verbal boxing as I recall was nothing but cross-examination: "Do you believe in the crucifixion of Jesus Christ?" "Yes, sir." "Do you believe in the resurrection of Jesus Christ?" Silence. "Well? Answer yes or no." "Does that matter?" "Definitely. Because this is the beginning of faith." "I admit Christianity is a great religion. And I admire Jesus Christ (*tatemae*). But . . . uh . . . when it comes to the resurrection story, mmm . . ." "That proves you are a man of little faith. I am in constant communication with Him through prayer." Put off, I was stuck for words, because I didn't know how I should translate into English my counterargument: "Is this your *honne*?"

Had I met a *hara*-logical man like Shusaku Endo earlier, however, I might have considered getting baptized right on the spot. So might many of my high school friends at that time. I admire the Christian missionary for his *hara* (uncompromising attitude) in *tatemae*, and at the same time dislike him for the lack of his *hara* (flexibility with which to tell *honne*). Torn between two contradictory feelings, here is the bottom line for the average Japanese: "Yes, we should give him credit in *tatemae*, but he is too *go-rippa* (unapproachably honest) for me to admire in *honne*." The notorious Japanese yes-but syndrome among non-Japanese is the product of Japanese *hara* culture.

Shumpei Kumon argues:

> Similarly no human laws, no elaborate clauses in human contracts, can cover the infinitely large variety of actual situations. For this reason all conceptual constructions such as theories, laws, etc., are destined to fail eventually in the face of reality. In this sense Japanese can be called "realists," because they never fully trust "logos," "principles," or "laws," either natural or human. According to their beliefs, so-called laws are not created by God but are artificially contrived by men through their limited power of reason. ("Some Principles Governing the Thought and Behavior of Japanists" in *The Journal of Japanese Studies*, Vol. 8 (1), Winter 1982)

Haragei contextualists say amen and give their counterdefinition of the beginning of the world: "In the beginning was the *ma*, and the *ma* was with humans and the *ma* was humans." And humans mean both *honne* and *tatemae* because of the *ma*. And, interestingly, it is no coincidence that the Japanese word "*ningen*" (human) means the *ma* (*gen*) of persons (*nin*). And more interestingly, the person's truth is the *ma* between *honne* and *tatemae*.

According to an opinion survey conducted by *Asahi Shimbun* in December 1981, 55 percent of those questioned answered in favor of the promotion of nuclear power and 23 percent in opposition; whereas to the question, "Do you favor the construction of a nuclear power plant near your house?" 24 percent changed their mind and answered negatively. The result is reversed as follows: Yes, 22%; No, 47%. Another example of how *tatemae* and *honne* come full circle can be found in the answers given to the following question on the above opinion survey: "Do you favor the increase in managerial positions for women?" Yes, 61%; No, 30%. "Do you want to work for a woman manager?" Yes, 22%; No, 56%.

Frustratingly, the national slogan of "Let's internationalize ourselves" can be situational because there has been no clash of arguments in Japan over either national or international principles. One tends to suspect that internationalization (*tatemae*) is another name for nationalism (*honne*) in view of the fact that "internationalization" has mostly been discussed in the context of the methods of the advancement of the international status or influence of Japan and the promotion of its national interests.

The Japanese tend to suspect any person who says openly, "I love my wife. You should give her the credit for my success," because they believe that it is only a *tatemae* statement and his *honne* ("I might have done a better job without her") is yet to be disclosed in a more private atmosphere. The safest *hara*-logical action is to say nothing (positive or negative) about your wife. When your husband is polite to you in public, better watch out.

B. *Dango*—A game the Japanese have never asked Americans to play

The maintenance of the Japanese *wa* (intra-group harmony or interpersonal harmony) calls for *hara*, because the *wa* exists not only among those who admire one another but among those who hate one another too. To play the everyone-must-be-happy game, every player must abide by the rules of the game of the ceremony. The unwritten rules of the ceremony game include:

1. Respect authority and tradition.
2. Be quiet.
3. Have *hara*.

Given the above rules, it would seem that American baseball players in the Japanese teams are the last players to be forced to play the game of the ceremony. Robert Whiting proves it by the following example: A former major-league all-star once arrived five days late for his second spring in Japan—because of a delay in visa processing—and discovered he had been fined the outrageous sum of $1000 for each day. Infuriated, he headed for the manager's office carrying the $4000 worth of American baseball equipment he had been asked to buy and demanded an explanation. There, behind closed doors, the following conversation took place.

American: (Indignantly) This is one hell of a way to start the season. I bring you all this equipment and now you're fining me? A thousand dollars a day? You've got to be kidding. I had visa problems that weren't my fault. I got here as fast as I could. Last year, I didn't get here until the middle of the month. So what's the fine for?

Manager: Now, now. Take it easy. Last year was different. You had permission then. Anyway, don't worry about the fine. I told the press that I was going to fine you, but I'm not going to do it.

American: That's a relief, but why announce it at all?

Manager: I did it for the other players, to show them I am in command. I'm the manager after all, and I have to show my power.

American: Yes, but what about my reputation?

Manager: I'm going to have to ask you to forget about your reputation. You must promise not to tell anyone what I have just told you. At the team meeting tomorrow, I'm going to announce your fine is being paid. You don't have to pay. The team will pay and we will use the money for the players' fund. But you must vow to keep this a secret.

American: You must be joking.

To synthesize the conflicts of interests or of personality, the ceremony must not be efficient but effective. The cozier the place is, the more the chances are for the performers to confirm each other's *honne*. This is one reason why in former times the tea room (*chaseki*) used to be chosen by military experts as an ideal site for exchanging highly confidential information. Today, however, the room of a high-class restaurant is preferred in order to synchronize the *honne* of the entertainer and the entertainee, while vital information is subtly traded.

If the meeting is conducted in a ceremonial fashion, there is no room for substantive discussion, much less clashes of arguments. The ceremonial meeting is designed first and foremost for *hanashiai* (prior consultation), or *dango* (a pre-arranged meeting to avoid embarrassment caused by unexpected events), in the context of, for example, competitive bidding among construction companies. *Dango* is considered a standard operating procedure in trade, although it is outlawed since it stifles fair competition.

However, what is stipulated in the law is not necessarily what is actually practiced. In Japan, we often hear people say, "Yes, that's what the law says in *tatemae*. But that's not the way it is (*Genjitsu wa chigau*)," in sharp contrast to the statement Americans make: "I'm sorry. But that's the law." As long as private construction companies beg for the services of influential retirees from public corporations (the practice called *amakudari*), not so much for what they can do in terms of job performance as for what their *kao* (influence) means to the companies, so *dango* as a means of maintaining *wa* will go on among those companies who can afford to hire highly-paid former government officials who bring "presents" (contracts). The *dango*-specialists, called "*dango ya*," play the role of a *gyoji* (referee) in sumo, whose job it is to bring participants onto the same "breathlength" (sumo jargon for synchronizing two *rikishi*'s breaths) on the ring called *dango*. And behind the *gyoji* stand *kuromaku* (black curtains) operating behind the scenes, so that each and every party concerned gets a piece of the action on a rotational basis. That is why the *dango* is often referred to as a chamber orchestra without a conductor.

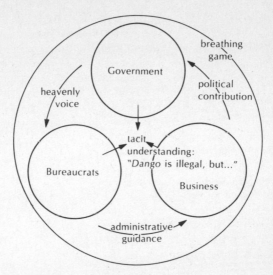

Figure 4   Breathing games to maintain the cozy
relationship within the triad.

Everyone knows *dango* is illegal. But the regulatory agencies treat the matter with benign neglect (*mekoboshi*) and the politicians look the other way because they are part of the breathing game. And strangely, regulations also breathe. Uninformed Westerners may develop the impression that the government, the bureaucrats, and the businesses are enjoying unsavory ties which often breed political scandals, as in the Lockheed trials. But the alliance is not so unholy as it seems. They are sumo wrestlers breathing on the circular *dohyo* ring. And they will do anything to maintain *wa* among themselves since they have a stake in the *wa* which is circular, as shown in Figure 4 and Figure 5.

What if a corporate executive is caught red-handed in the act of *dango* dealing? Don't worry. Corporate executives may be dragged into the Diet and forced to testify before the congress and a television audience. But they will refuse to tell the truth

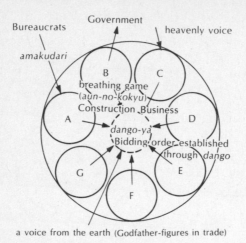

a voice from the earth (Godfather-figures in trade)

Figure 5   Consensus among competitors
(or non-competitors?) through *dango*

even when they are under oath, swallowing their pride as in both the Lockheed and the Grumman scandal cases. Why can those big fish get away with staying mum or uttering "Sssaaa" or other grunts and groans and enduring the ordeal of eating crow, tantamount in pain to *hara-kiri*? The reason is simple: They stood on the *suji* principle by protecting the interests of their company and the vested interests of still bigger fish (fixers, bureaucrats, and politicians who usually go scot-free). It was a test of *hara*.

Ask most Japanese what they think of *dango*, and you will get their "Sssaaa." And if you play the devil's advocate to get the truth out of them, they will get uncomfortable and say bluntly, "Which truth do you want, *tatemae* or *honne*?"

C. *Oyabun*: Men of big *hara* and *haragei*

Oyabun, a man who's got it all together. What do you get when you get it all together: *hara*? *Gei*? You will be looked upon as an ideal *oyabun* in any male organization in Japan. *Oyabun* is not exactly the kind of tough guy that usually engenders a negative connotation in Western Society; rather it includes the positive denotation of a big-hearted leader surrounded by a bunch of loyal *kobun* (*oyabun*'s male subordinates). *A Japanese boss willing to sacrifice his own interests for his men or look the other way when they make mistakes is referred to as a man of Hara.* An *oyabun*, or a man of big *hara*, is usually the recipient of attention, respect and love, both in and out of the office, due to his well-rounded, empathetic kind of leadership.

Will Western managers in foreign-owned companies in Japan be able to learn the Art of *oyabun*ship?

Yes, but at their own risk. In order to understand the depth and breadth of the risk one ought to take a scrutinizing look at the *oyabun*'s list of attributes (familiarization with them might even convince the daredevil Western manager to think carefully before daring to play the *oyabun* game). Who knows, the real non-tariff barriers in Japan may be "*haragei*" and "*oyabun*ship."

1. *Oyabun* don't try to win. To win, one must be aggressive. Yet, to be aggressive goes against the principle of *wa* (group harmony). Then how can you win the hearts and minds of your subordinates (hereinafter referred to as *kobun*) in Japan?

In Japan, the rule of the game is often what you win is what you lose, so *oyabun* do not play a zero-sum game. They often do verbal judo (the gentle art). They rarely come on strong, preferring to wait for the attack, and turn it around in their favor. *So it appears that it pays to lose.* The question is, when and how to lose?

There are times when you must win, to prove you have what it takes to be called an *oyabun*. Win what, if not their hearts or minds? Their *hara*. Let me explain. Hearts and minds, like emotions and logic, god and devil, have been the products of the

Western dichotomy since ancient Greece. The mind and heart contradict each other whereas *hara*, the least understood part of the human anatomy in the Western society, does not contradict anything. The *hara*, being contradictory in nature just "stomachs" everything, including conflicts. "Ha ha ha. You win and I lose. Do as you see fit—and accept the consequence." *Oyabun* can get away with this. They never lose as long as they choose to lose.

It takes a big guy to really understand the *hara* of a big guy. A Japanese man of *hara* might play an *oyabun* game with his Western boss. "Well, before you fire my men, fire me first," as is often the case with the Japanese bosses who consider it chic to threaten to fire themselves in the spirit of self-denial.

It takes a manager of mind to say, "That's easy. You're fired." (I know numerous such examples.)

A manager of heart says: "I'm sorry. I really am. But you leave me no choice. I'll accept your resignation."

An *oyabun* says: "I'm sorry. It's my responsibility. I'll fire myself. I know you've been taking care of your men, buying them drinks out of your pocket. Let me pay the price this time. You take care of my boys (*kobun*) after I'm gone."

A tough act to follow, isn't he?

Your man will immediately fall under your spell and follow you like a shadow thereafter. It's a high-risk, high-return art. But with his firm *hara*, he accepts either decision, favorable or unfavorable. His *hara* action is that of so-called "male romanticism" in Japan, and its emotional interaction comes under tear-jerking *naniwa-bushi* sentimentalism. *Naniwabushi* (emotional drama) still works in Japanese corporate culture, because nobody wins and nobody loses. It's the chemistry that brings together the leaders, their followers and their bona fide onlookers. To win in the Japanese corporate culture is science; not to win is an art.

2. *Oyabun* do not cause their men (*kobun*) to lose face.

Many Americans wondering why Asia is more successful economically than other Third World areas such as Latin America or Africa, suspect that what they call Confucian capitalism (Hong

Kong, Korea, Taiwan and Singapore) works better. It is worth noting that Japan, being part of Confucian capitalism in the eyes of Westerners, still stresses the importance of face saving in business transactions and people management.

The most humiliating punishment a group-serving businessman, *oyabun* or *kobun*, can get is to be singled out and embarrassed as a self-server. *Oyabun* dare not single out an unfortunate *kobun* for punishment. The *oyabun* simply "stomachs" the incident away or takes the blame himself in public in the form of "*otoshimae*" (a *yakuza*'s method of voluntarily accepting the consequences caused by his *kobun* by means of symbolically cutting off his little finger). With his lost finger, the *oyabun* gains credit from the insiders for what he has done ... preventing his *kobun* from losing face and losing the trust of outsiders.

Businessmen, like *yakuza* today, don't cut off their fingers. They do "resign to take responsibility," the way Toshiba's top executives have done to apologize for the violations of COCOM principles. Yet, the *otoshimae* mentality of the traditional *yakuza* still goes on in the minds of Japanese *oyabun* managers, to maintain the integrity of the masculine Japanese corporations. The question remains: Did Toshiba management apologize out of *hara* (toughness) or out of *amae* (softness)? The answer depends on whose face is lost and whose is saved.

3. *Oyabun* do not explain.

The most successful companies in Japan are usually manned by taciturn *oyabun* executives and hardly by verbally assertive executives who demand explanations all the time. The *oyabun* managers get the kind of loyal followership they deserve.

The small-time *oyabun*, or bosses of small *hara*, demand explanations from their men more than is necessary.

"Why do you need to privately borrow money so badly now?"

"I can't say, sir."

"Explain."

"Medical expense."

"Shame on you. Here's the money."

(A non-*oyabun*'s answer would be a straight no. Or rather, small-*hara* bosses would probably not get such private requests in the first place.)

The typical big-time *oyabun*'s reaction would be like this:

"What? You want me to loan you money? Take it."

"I hate to . . . eh . . . ."

"Don't explain."

If he's heard the reason already, he might say, "I didn't hear it."

Accepting his *kobun*'s request only *after* hearing his explanation limits his sphere of action and gets only his partial loyalty, whereas giving him what he wants *without* hearing his explanation invites his loyalty and *samurai* dedication.

It is the intense internal competition among corporate *oyabun* with big enough *hara* not to demand explanation during private consultations that makes excellent companies excellent. *Oyabun* seldom explain anymore than the ancient *samurai* did.

Tetsu Aiko, President of Daiei U.S.A., Inc., explains: I can easily get into the *hara* of my boss (Ko Nakauchi). And when I negotiate with American businessmen, I usually sit back and listen, not that I don't like to speak English. I let my trusted spokesman negotiate the way he likes and act according as he interprets my implicit message. And very often I wonder why chief American negotiators want to explain and decide by themselves.

4. *Oyabun* do not act first.

One of the quickest ways to get the feel of Japanese society is to learn its language. But being able to speak Japanese does not necessarily mean being able to communicate in it. Frustration sets in when a foreign manager begins to speak Japanese. "The more fluent I become, the more I am made to feel an alien. The Japanese expect me to remain a *gaijin* (outsider) who can speak only English. Why?"

How many times have I heard blue-eyed *gaijin* say this? Are they paranoid? "Yes, I am paranoid," says one of those frustrated *gaijin* who speaks embarrassingly beautiful Japanese. "You Japanese will never internationalize yourselves as long as you expect *gaijin* to be *gaijin.*"

He is right. Those Japanese who think in terms of *we* and *they* are those of small *hara*. By the same token, those Westerners who insist we Japanese speak Japanese because we are Japanese or because we are in Japan are also of small *hara*.

An *oyabun* may refuse to use a foreign language and let his men speak for him even when he knows he can speak it. Why? Because he puts his men ahead of him according to the logic of the situation rather than his own logic or perspective. He listens first and talks second. He speaks *your* language, not *his*. This kind of *kikubari* or thoughtful attention to the needs of others is required of any *oyabun* in Japan. *Oyabun* are not John Waynes or Burt Lancasters. *Oyabun*, like hawks, hide their claws. *Oyabuns* are reactors. Acting means putting yourself ahead of others; reacting means putting others ahead of yourself. In Japan, where patience is the name of the game, one must learn the art of reacting. Even a decisive Imperialist leader such as Takamori Saigo was a reactor, because he decided at the very last moment not to burn Edo (now called Tokyo)—reacting to Kaishu Katsu, representative of the Tokugawa Shogunate who in turn was busily reacting to Saigo's *hara*. The historic conflict that brought about the win-win situation was resolved through *haragei*. The absence of verbal action involved between them at that *crucial* time, attests to the validity of the reacting aspect of *haragei* as a method of crisis management. Even sworn enemies react to each other to prove themselves *oyabun*, through the tough tests of *hara*.

5. *Oyabun* do not think and act in a straight line.

Logic, since Socrates, is mind-centered. It goes straight and linearly. Visceral logic goes circularly. The majority of Orientals, particularly Japanese, are circularly (*hara*)—logical. Straight logic goes like this: every successful boss needs efficient secretaries, and I am an efficient secretary because I am the fastest typist in class, therefore you need me. Now, using circular logic: "I am you.

You are me. I think I'm not qualified for the secretarial job. What do you think? You decide, Sir."

Non sequitur? It may not be *the* logic, but it is *a* logic. Talking straight stifles the *"ma,"* or pregnant pause. Talking specifically to a point in front of an audience is *ma*-less and therefore *efficient* because everyone gets the same message, but talking around the point is *ma*-full *and thus effective because everyone is expected to get the very message he or she must get.* It takes *oyabun* to listen circularly and to read between and beyond the lines when *kobun* talk circularly. *Oyabun* are prone to subtle exchanges of poetic messages; *"Yappari* (after all), the sun and the moon are different." Is he talking about the management (the sun) and labor (the moon)? Or is he talking about my family (mini-universe) or me (the sun) and my wife (the moon playing the sun)? Is he merely talking about his pet Yin-Yang theory applicable to people management? Nobody understands his real message unless it is analyzed circularly. The worst crime is argumentation, because straight logic employed in intellectual argumentation helps make messages clearer, therefore sharpening conflicts.

Who knows, the listener might get the wrong idea and conclude that when husband and wife vie for the powerful position of the sun, something has to give. So what? Right or wrong, they will get the message: "Educate your wife so she can fit in." And that's what *oyabun* want eventually. *Oyabun* do not "push" their ideas; but they expect their men to "pull" out (or extract) their *oyabun*'s ideas or unspoken messages.

This is how the mammoth manufacturing empire of Matsushita (National Panasonic) is run. Japanese masculine financial institutions (Nomura Securities and Sumitomo Bank) are the same. Emotions and caring (*omoiyari*) go a long way toward getting familial feelings going at your office in Japan. Most important, caring must be shown and hopefully not explained logically. The more logical your message, the more deceptive it often looks. *Oyabun* play the father in office and play the mother out of office or vice versa, depending on the development of the situations.

Oyabun must "understand" each situation as it varies. Each situation deserves each truth, *and logic only serves to give the moment's truth an identity* as of that particular moment, an identity that needs to be redefined at the following moment.

6. *Oyabun* do not solve problems.

Aloof Europeans, complex Russians and visceral Japanese tend to view Americans as a single-minded people who hope that every problem has a single solution and can be solved if they want it to be. The fact of the matter is, there is no problem-free situation. Big companies have big-company problems. Small companies have small-company problems. True *oyabun* dare to look nonchalant when a problem occurs, though this does not imply that they wink at it.

A great number of major corporations in Japan climbed onto the bandwagon of American-born quality circles so enthusiastically, as part of an intra-company effort to solve such problems as sagging morale or declining productivity, that they eventually developed the concept of Total Quality Circles, a Japanese version of the original American Quality Circles. The spirit of the holistic Total Quality Circles goes hand in hand with the *oyabun's* value-free, hands-off policy. *Oyabun*, understanding human nature, know that pushing their ideas down their men's throats would have a demoralizing effect. Does it work? Yes, if *oyabun's* *hara* is big enough he can wait till the problems solve themselves. Men of small *hara* attempt to fight the problems as they come up and end up fighting another problem. Men of big *hara* "befriend the problems, rather than antagonizing them." If MBAs make efficient managers, *oyabun* make effective leaders and followers. To *oyabun*, every conflict is an opportunity to prove how effectively they can "stomach" it and develop their *hara*. *Oyabun* would refuse to solve minor problems one at a time. The size of an *oyabun's* *hara* makes or breaks the Total Quality Circle. Will American bosses make it work in Japan? Ask their *hara*.

7. *Oyabun* do not manage.

A manager's business for all intents and purposes is to manage. Keeping your group or organization together *without anybody managing* is an ideal method of management since non-management means giving nature a free hand. *Oyabun* know when to manage and when not to manage their *kobun*. *Oyabun* refuse to be fenced in by job descriptions; they create job descriptions as the scope of their activity expands. The real *oyabun*, whether he be a chief executive officer or director or even a section chief, knows the knack of supervising bosses above them while babysitting their own *kobun*. Babysitting his men? Yes. Playing godfather to their men means shouldering their responsibility that often extends over into their private life when the need arises. In other words, *oyabun* accept their *kobun* whole, their strengths and weaknesses. If your totality (*hara*) holds your *kobun* under your spell, is there any further need to manage? Your men, face saved, will cry "male tears" and be your loyal *kobun*. Big boys, too, cry in Japan. Nobody manages. Nobody is managed.

8. *Oyabun* do not get soft with insiders.

Oyabun are in firm control of their invisible *hara*, a center of human anatomy. But their minds and hearts are shaky like leaves on a tree. They set up strategy based on their *hara*, but when it comes to tactic-setting to support their strategy, they must rely on their minds or hearts.

Oyabun are agile and adapt to change so swiftly that they give others an impression that they are temperamental or unprincipled.

An *oyabun* may suddenly change his mind and say,

"Get the guy into my company."

"You mean, employing the man who once betrayed you, sir."

"Yes."

"Why?"

"Because I like him."

Oyabun feel no qualms about getting outsiders in, nor in getting insiders out. *Oyabun* viscerally understand the dangers inherent in over-democratization and bureaucratization within their office. The worst potential enemy within is the one closest to them. That is why *oyabun* get tougher with the blood-related *kobun* or their other relatives at the risk of appearing tyrannical. It takes their heart to protect their blood-related confidants under their wings; but it takes *hara* to keep them at arms length.

Oyabun are always the sun, radiating solar energy to the planets of *kobun* that surround him. The sun must be in the center of the solar system and never at the mercy of the planetary movement.

9. *Oyabun* do not get credit first.

It is human nature (heart) to wish to receive credit (where credit is due?) for the kind of employee management that results in various and sundry accomplishments. However the accumulation of such credit, in Japan at least, can be quite like a double-edged sword; on the one hand ensuring a rapid climb up the corporate totem pole, while on the other bringing with it the insecurity of abrupt and sudden falls.

Oyabun refuse to take credit ahead of their *kobun*. It takes self-disciplined *hara* to resist the temptation of letting your emotions get in the way of long range decision making and policy setting.

Oyabun wait. Their *hara* "buys them time." Mind is usually short term. Heart is mid-term. But *hara* is long term. *Hara* demands that you wait until your *kobun* of their own initiative promote you. *Hara*, being impartial by nature, also demands that your *kobun* begin promoting you by giving you the credit for the job that they know is theirs.

Seldom do *oyabun* criticize their *kobun* openly. But they occasionally do show anger, castigating their *kobun* in front of others. If, and when, this happens, they try to compensate privately. Konosuke Matsushita is known as the master of both public scolding (*shikarikata no meijin*) and private ego-soothing. *Oyabun* know how to verbally criticize their *kobun* (*shikarikata*) and *kobun* know how to take the criticism. *Kobun* of big *hara* must learn the art of being verbally assaulted or scolded (*shikararekata*) to prove they have the makings (*utsuwa* or vessel) of becoming potential *oyabun*.

To receive criticism openly is an opportunity for a *kobun* to have his *hara* sized up. If he *shows* displeasure or defends himself, saying, "I'm not the only one responsible for a mistake. It's everybody's mistake," or "You should've told me earlier. Why now?" It proves he has a small *hara*—a man of small vessel (*utsuwa no chiisai otoko*). *Oyabun* don't give advice piecemeal; they just erupt like a volcano when their *hara* says enough is enough.

Oyabun wait, wait and wait, until the right moment comes to really blurt out their pent-up anger, having deliberately let a series of minor errors pass by ostensibly undetected.

Oyabun criticize deductively from the basic attitudinal errors responsible for the syndrome. An *oyabun* of big *hara* might say to his error-prone man, "You're 'feminist' (meaning in Japan 'partial to women'), aren't you? Ha, ha, ha . . ."

The message must be understood by *hara* alone. "Umm, the boss wants me to get together with my wife. Come to think of it, the series of my mistakes he's overlooked comes from my weak-kneed attitude toward my family members." Any *oyabun* of lesser *hara* explains the reason for his criticism, or on the other hand reductively, from examples to basics, at the risk of getting refuted evidence, by his men of small *hara*, imparts his feelings.

Only small *hara* superiors criticize their men piecemeal, lest they incur criticism from above for not having controlled their men by chewing them out "properly" (meaning each time an error is flagrantly evident).

Criticizing their men each time they notice an error can justify their role as boss. But the other side of the coin is clearly that constant nitpicking makes their men "good soldiers" at best, perfect cogs in the "inhuman" corporate machine at worst.

Oyabun want creative men capable of becoming big *oyabun* in the future, so they pick the right time and place to really give it to their men at the level of *hara*.

The *oyabun* who has caused his *kobun* to lose face in public loses the credit himself because everyone says the *oyabun* has not the *hara* to control his emotions. However, the *kobun* receives credit for "stomaching" his humiliation. Did the *oyabun* lose? On the contrary, the *oyabun* got tough and got what he wanted, letting other members of the family (or office) get the message that no one, not even his beloved *kobun*, can take him for granted. This is a variation of *haragei* called the art of "outstomaching" others.

10. *Oyabun* do not dance on stage.

Dancing on stage attracts a lot of attention; dancing off stage does not. On stage, you must dance to a tune; off stage you can dance to your own tune. Tough guys in America do not dance, but *oyabun* in Japan do dance off stage. *Oyabun* dance and get their *kobun* to dance to their tunes.

Oyabun love socializing; singing and dancing are part of their stock in trade. They do not whisper. They speak loudly. They do not titter. They belly laugh. They know how and when to switch off. The corporate *oyabun* can be called daytime capitalists and nighttime socialists. They act uninhibited at the private meetings they sponsor and encourage their *kobun* to pull out all the stops once in a while. They do not write books. They write scenarios. They do not seek publicity on television. They do not dance on stage. They dance off stage. They stage manage, wheeling and dealing and grinning behind the scenes.

It is these *oyabun*-types that the chief executive officers want to keep around as their right-hand men. It is these *oyabun* who make excellent executive strategists (*sambo*) or stage managers, who make other *oyabun* bosses dance the way they want.

III

WHERE DOES *HARAGEI* COME FROM?

Although variations of *haragei* may be found to exist in other parts of the world, there is nothing like the *haragei* performed in the racially homogeneous Japanese society. Having never been long under the rule of foreign powers that destroyed its national polity (*kokutai*), Japan fortunately or unfortunately has not lost its homogeneity or what some Japanese call "racial purity." In an extremely high-context culture like Japan's, where simple messages with deep meaning flow freely, what one feels is what others feel. Intuitive understanding, which is one of the building blocks of *haragei*, is the by-product of such a homogeneous culture. This does not mean, however, that any homogeneous society is inherently capable of nurturing *haragei*. For example, in Amish society, religious conformity is so strictly enforced that there seems to be no room for *haragei* to emerge. Yet the fact remains that homogeneity is undoubtedly one of the conditions for *haragei* development, since tacit understanding, a prerequisite for *haragei* action, better serves the purpose of communication where so much is taken for granted or understood. *Haragei* is also indebted to other cultural determinants, like Shintoism, Japanese mythology, Buddhism, Zen, and the Japanese climate. These are its possible roots.

A. Shinto has served as the cornerstone for two important *haragei* rules: total acceptance, and purity in motives.

Shinto, the way of the gods, is a way of embracing reality characterized by non-duality. There has been no historical parallel for what Westerners call identity. Spirit and matter used to be grasped as inseparable. Shinto claims no official dogma or sacred scriptures. Such central concepts as *kami* (deities), *musubi* (creating and harmonizing power), *makoto* (truthfulness), and *harai* (purification) are integrated into the total Shinto way of life and worship. Shinto has imparted its tolerant and accepting attitude to *haragei's* value-free orientation. One's *hara* must be "pure" to accept another's mind as it is, as does Shinto. There can be no power games in a nature-to-nature communication. Shinto does not seek dominance over Buddhism or Confucianism; it merely co-exists with them as nature does. Shinto itself is compulsively receptive in nature and rejects nothing, though Shintoists may not be so open. The readiness to swallow the pure with the impure (*seidaku awase nomu*) required of men of *hara* has its roots in Shinto and is considered to be what it takes to be a qualified *haragei* practitioner. Such Shintoist open-mindedness, or broad-mindedness, made it possible for the ancient Japanese to accept seven popular deities of different nationalities for their popular worship, known as Shichi-fuku-jin (Seven Lucky Gods). The notion of the "chosen Gods" would sound appallingly sacrilegious to Westerners' ears, unless they possess big enough *hara* to compromise their *tatemae* (surface principle). The readiness to accept things as they are and as they come lends itself to the concept of *sunao*, or obedience, that abhors critical attitudes.

Don Maloney, a former American businessman in Japan, says that the Japanese never think about whys. The why-askers tend to be frowned upon as not being *sunao* ("non-resistant" or "non-suspicious"), a highly prized virtue in Japan. When a famous professor sends letters to prestigious Japanese corporations asking for monetary support for the maintenance of "Japanese studies" in one of the major American universities, the recipient, perhaps a head of a general affairs section, will say, "Who (other corporations in the same industry) else?" instead of "Why?"

The awkwardness of the Japanese when confronted with "why" questions, stems partly from the Japanese tendency to react *sunaoni* or non-critically. The culturally determined orientation is that of accepting a situation as it presents itself. And this is where *sunao* and *hara* merge, in that they both approve of and reject nothing. Konosuke Matsushita, a moral leader in Japanese business management and an advocate of the Way of Man, preaches *sunao*, but this does not mean he does not ask why. He argues that we must look at man as he is—with his good and bad sides—and accept the duality (Konosuke Matsushita, *Thoughts on Man*, PHP Institute International, Inc., 1981). What he preaches in essence is to develop *hara*. The nebulous quality of *hara* makes it possible to be naive like a dove and suspicious like a serpent. Have *hara* will travel in Japan—because a man who is both *sunao* and non-*sunao* at the same time is an embodiment of nature.

Since the average housewife or schoolteacher tends to consider *sunao* the chief educational philosophy to impart to the young, children are raised in a *sunao* fashion. The teachers' ready answer as to the specific method of bestowing a *sunao* attitude is: "One, getting the children to say 'I'm sorry' readily; and two, getting them to say 'thank you' automatically, to anybody for anything," thus maintaining *wa* (group harmony among themselves).

Sunao-ness is encouraged throughout one's life. *Sunao-na-okusan* is translated as an obedient and docile wife. Although it carries a negative connotation when translated into English, in Japanese culture it is considered virtuous. *Sunao*, in other words, means not asking why. *Sunao-de-nai* (non-*sunao*) American baseball players on Japanese teams who ask "why?" are often considered the destroyers of *wa* and can expect trouble in interpersonal dealings in Japan. *Sunao-de-nai-okusan* ("disobedient" wives) say "*datte*" (which usually means "but" and is followed by a situation given as the reason for not doing something). "*Datte shikata ga nai mono*" (but, there's nothing I can do about it) is an effective female tactic of verbal self-defense.

To inhibit any inclinations diverting one from *sunao*, the influence of *seken-no-me* (eyes of neighbors) or societal pressure is felt almost instinctively. This, coupled with the concept of group thinking, weighs heavily on the developing mind and quiets the question "why" that children are so apt to ask.

By the time Japanese children reach the age of sensitivities, the cultural parallel for the age of reason (to be explained in more detail later), they are aware of the needs and inklings of neighbors. This gives rise to the controversial Japanese version of situational ethics: *honne* and *tatemae*.

Tatemae is the spoken gesture of avowed maintenance of harmony with outsiders, while *honne* is honest feelings among insiders. The former is *wa* without, whereas the latter is *wa* within. Preserving *tatemae* is the basis of preserving *wa* both within and without. The *haragei* master understands where *honne* begins and *tatemae* leaves off and utilizes them as befits the situation. The situation becomes more important than rigid principles. A seasoned or mature person can stretch the truth in accordance with the logic of the situation and, as a practical matter, the practice called "*uso-mo-hoben*" or "situationally acceptable untruth" works. This should not be equated with dishonesty or an attempt at deception, but rather a *haragei* practitioner's exercise in group harmony.

B. Japan's climate made *haragei* obscure and situational.

The climate of Japan is characterized by a variety of seasons. The Japanese concept of nature is expressed by the notion of *mujokan* (evanescence); the only thing constant is change.

Mujokan is exemplified by the characteristic Japanese custom of enjoying the cherry blossoms. The Japanese identify with the blossoms not just because they are beautiful but because their beauty is shortlived, and therefore epitomizes the fragility of beauty. Detached, the cherry is just a tree; attached, it is as human as we are.

A glance at the thousand-odd years of Japanese literature will confirm the significance of another aspect of nature in the Japanese world-view: the moon. Daisetsu Suzuki draws a connection between the Japanese predilection for softness and suggestiveness and their fondness for the moon. For the Japanese, it is a moon partially obscured by clouds that is the most appealing. Its light is gentle and subtle, leaving objects in a cloud of dim obscurity. It is understandable that people with such an aesthetic makeup would resist the bright, the clear, or the obvious.

This obscurity exists in the atmospheric conditions of Japan as well. Much of the year the landscape is enveloped in mist. It is inevitable that such an environment would produce the sensitivity to see through the dim light and beyond the shadows. Political scandals are usually called "kuroi kiri" or black mists. With each revelation of a politico-business scandal, haragei is given a bad name. It might be of some interest to compare the starkly different messages below: the clear statement by an American senator and the misty memorandum by a Japanese government official.

You have to deal with barbarians as barbarians.
    —Senator William Mangum of North Carolina, on the Perry Mission

I am therefore convinced that our policy should be to stake everything on the present opportunity, to conclude friendly alliances, to send ships to foreign countries everywhere and conduct trade, to copy the foreigners where they are at their best and so repair our own shortcomings, to foster our national strength and complete our armaments, and so gradually subject the foreigners to our influence until in the end all the countries of the world know the blessings of perfect tranquility and our hegemony is acknowledged throughout the globe.
    —Hotta Masayoshi's memorandum on foreign policy
            (circa December 1857)
        (As We Saw Them by Masao Miyoshi)

Japan is plagued by the annual visits of typhoons that play havoc with crops. Yet these same typhoons assure a good harvest. Japanese accept as a fact of life the continuous changes that are brought with nature, and so do not dwell on the obvious destruction caused by the typhoons. The Japanese feel comfortable with the notion that nature is situational and that man is situational, and at the same time, *kami* (gods) are situational toward both man and nature. Since *hara* is situational and unpredictable in nature, it is common knowledge that it takes *hara* to accept change as it comes, as well as the obscurity that situations bring about.

This leads other nationalities to wonder if situational Japanese have a set of principles. Professor Yasuo Wakatsuki, author of *Siberian Prisoner of War Camps*, laments the Japanese lack of principles.

"However, this advantage on the part of Japanese is two-edged, for it becomes a weakness when an emergency or crisis arises. Recently I published a book on records from World War II concerning some 600,000 Japanese soldiers who were held in Russian prisoner of war camps in Siberia. While going through the volumes of documents, I felt most miserable to learn of the extent of the gutlessness of Japanese under extreme conditions although the hardships these men had to undergo in these camps, under the atrocious policy of the Soviet government, were certainly of no usual kind."

Strangely enough, many scholars in Japan subscribe to the theory of Professor Chie Nakane of Tokyo University that the Japanese have no principles. Stranger still, not a single Japanese that I have heard of was surprised by Professor Nakane's contradictory statement at the Foreign Correspondents' Club of Japan that the Japanese have many principles. Obviously the above two statements contradict each other, but according to Japanese *hara*-logic they are both correct and incorrect, neither is simply correct or incorrect. For the correct answer, if you insist, listen to the wind.

A famous Japanese *haiku* reads, "Matsushima ya, Ah, Matsushima ya, Matsushima ya." Hundreds of interpretations are possible. And yet the Japanese teachers of *kokugo* (national language) expect their pupils to write an interpretation of the possible feelings of the poet. To read into the ah-ness of the poet is not easy unless one uses *hara* instead of mind, because "ah" could mean a hundred different things depending on the context.

I was not able to leave the breathtakingly beautiful Taj Mahal without sporting a somewhat parodial poem of Basho's in my travel log; applying a little of the "ah" myself that is,

Taj Mahal, *ah* Taj Mahal, Taj Mahal

This *ah* is very pregnant with meaning. So full of it that I fear its misinterpretation (over or under exaggerated that is) by "poor *hara*" readers. The result is my own uncharacteristically overemphasized English translation:

YOU are beautiful Taj Mahal
You ARE beautiful Taj Mahal
You are BEAUTIFUL Taj Mahal

And then to extend to somewhere beyond surface impressions and feelings:

IT is beautiful, Taj Mahal
It IS beautiful, Taj Mahal
Is it REALLY beautiful, Taj Mahal?

My diary of May 11, 1987 reads as follows:

"Thought aloud. What's great about the King Shah Jahan? He, like everyone else, mourned the death of the queen. And he built a memorial to his loved one. But did it make her happy? Really happy? The king ordered his chief mason's right hand to be cut off to make sure he would make no copy of the beautiful building. Is it a universal love or a gesture of benevolence?"

The interpretation of Japanese poets' "ah" is risky. The meditative murmurings on the magnificence of Matsushima are best compared to the following poem about Athens which enjoys almost 300 days of bright sunshine a year:

Athens lies like a sapphire in the earth's ring.
Light is everywhere, all is light,
and everything is by the light revealed.

Dr. Helen Theodoropoulos, a Greek professor of literature, describes Greece as "a country without noteworthy natural resources, but whose climate, the temperateness and sea, contribute to the intellectual lucidity of its inhabitants and to the development of an immortal civilization."

A misty country like Japan which abounds in ambiguity, accompanied by a changeable climate, can hardly contribute to clarity of thought. While the ancient Greeks believed that unity and order came out of chaos, "a yawning void," the Japanese have successfully preserved the chaos and developed the void into a highly polished art of human interaction called *haragei*.

C. Buddhism contributed a "human" quality to *haragei*.

"Buddhism is the teaching ascribed to Gautama Buddha, holding that suffering is inherent in life and that one can escape it into nirvana by mental and moral self-purification." (*Webster's International Dictionary*) A Buddha is not a transcendental God; he is a human being. Basically everyone, Karlfried Dürckheim proclaims, is what the Buddha expresses, and in the course of his development, can grow into Buddha.

Pure reality or nirvana—rest, harmony, and an unchanging being—can be experienced only when the futility of all conceptual thinking is recognized. To attain nirvana means to enter the void (*sunyata*). Voidness is not mere nothingness, but is the very source of all life and the essence of all forms. It resembles *hara*, since it means the absence of ego. In *hara*, the difference between "we" and "they" disappears as in the marriage between Shinto and Buddhism (*Shinbutsu Shugo*). It is hardly surprising in Japan to hear a sob sister offering a friendly bit of advice to a 27-year-old housewife complaining about her husband's never-ending affair with a 34-year-old bar hostess (a true story): "I suggest you have *hara.*" The popular Catholic novelist, Shusaku Endo, suggests husbands do not divorce their wives no matter how hard their life is because Jesus carried a cross by himself bearing human suffering. What logic? Is his advice Shintoist, Buddhist, or Christian? But the fact remains that anything he says rings "human" to the followers of Endo's religion and is acceptable.

Critic Shichihei Yamamoto calls this unique religious phenomenon in Japan "human religion," in contrast to the "God religion" of the West. Anything that a master of *haragei* says goes and is followed religiously in Japan, as long as it smacks of human suffering and empathy: a Buddhist country by sentiment.

D. Zen's artistic orientation brought about the rapprochement between *hara* and art: *haragei.*

Zen, albeit an offshoot of Buddhism, remains a religion beyond religion, or more precisely, a teaching without words, without explanations, without instructions, and without knowledge. It is a shift from the cognitive to the intuitive. Zen is not interested in any abstraction or conceptualization; rather its emphasis is on naturalness and spontaneity—a discipline in perfecting the original nature. A man of *hara* is pragmatic rather than dogmatic, contradictory rather than organized, unorthodox rather than orthodox, artistic rather than scientific, implicit rather than explicit, and intuitive rather than logical.

The four principles of the Zen sect are as follows:

1) No dependence on words and letters (*furyumonji*)
2) The transmission of truth which is beyond the scriptures (*kyogebetsuden*)
3) Direct emphasis on the soul of man (*chokushijinshin*)
4) Achieving insight into one's nature is the attainment of Buddhahood (*kenshojobutsu*).

Haragei is a highly polished art in human interaction, best performed with inner maturity or *shibumi*. The master of *hara* is a master of more than technique—he has mastered *shibumi* in himself. Practice is needed before *shibui* (adjective for *shibumi*) *haragei* can be performed—a performance from the deepest level without intellectualizing one's actions. *Shibumi*, literally astringency, is eloquently described by Trevanian, author of the best-seller *Shibumi*.

"Oh, vaguely. And incorrectly, I suspect. A blundering attempt to describe an ineffable quality. As you know, *shibumi* has to do with great refinement underlying commonplace appearances. It is a statement so correct that it does not have to be bold, so poignant it does not have to be pretty, so true it does not have to be real. *Shibumi* is understanding, rather than knowledge. Eloquent silence. In demeanor, it is modesty without pudency. In art, where the spirit of *shibumi* takes the form of *sabi*, it is elegant simplicity, articulate brevity. In philosophy, where *shibumi* emerges as *wabi*, it is spiritual tranquility that is not passive; it is being without the angst of becoming. And in the personality of a man, it is . . . how does one say it? Authority without domination? Something like that, sir?"

The "something like that" is hard to achieve unless one has reached the autumn or winter stage of life as explained earlier. One does not develop *shibumi* easily; *shibumi* develops itself. However, constant practice accelerates the development of *shibumi* as in art or in *haragei*. A man of *shibumi* is a man of developed *hara*. A man of undeveloped *hara* may try to put on a *haragei* act to display his *shibumi* but this will surely end up with his being called a spoilsport. *Shibumi*, if and when developed, "communicates" by itself. Zen has no need to externalize things, but art has. By the same token, *hara* has no wish for revelation, but *gei* (art) feels itself within its duty to externalize it. *Haragei*, thus, is Zen in disguise.

This is the very reason why *haragei* remains bafflingly mysterious in the eyes of logical-minded people including Japanese. I can imagine why they easily throw up their hands in despair, saying, "The question is totally illogical. How can I describe the voice of the baby that is not born yet?" Perhaps they are referring to the seemingly nonsensical riddles, *koan*, which Dr. Fritjof Capra asserts are meant to make the student of Zen realize the limitation of

logic and reasoning in a most dramatic way. The irrational wording and paradoxical content of these riddles make it impossible
to solve them by thinking. They are designed precisely to stop
the thought process and thus to make the student ready for the
non-verbal experience of reality (*Tao of Physics*, by Fritjof Capra,
Bantam, page 35).

The Zen puzzle (*koan*) is perhaps the most sublimated form of
traditional communication/non-communication in Japan, because Zen, if viewed in an objective light, is a logical way of dis-
crediting logic. Contradiction-bound *haragei* borders on the Zen
relativism that emphasizes the non-duality of form and substance and the identity of form and spirit (the essence of art).

The development of the hearts and minds through education is
not easy. But far more difficult is the attempt to develop students'
hara, which by nature discards the trainer-trainee dichotomy. As
explained earlier by the burglar story, giving *hara*-development
training is not only difficult but involves risk. For myself, I have
taken calculated risks in corporate debate-training seminars by
forcing all trainees to sit in a lotus position (*zazen*) before debate
matches begin, while I instruct them: "Forget about winning the
debate. Get thoughts out. Concentrate." And when I see some-
body sway for lack of concentration I hit him hard with a bamboo
sword, or literally shake up the group by my roaring "voice" warning stick so they get out all their thoughts and feelings (pain included). After the tortuous *zazen*, everyone bows and shouts from
the diaphragm, "*Arigato gozaimashita* (Thank you)!" Thoughts
come back, more energized. The trainees get back to work, to add
the finishing touches to their debate strategy. It works. Sometimes I give them a *koan*, such as: "Can you see other people's
breathing?"—not to confuse them but to sharpen their creativity
through their turned-on *hara*. But I often forget to ask them for
answers later, and they forget that too. So be it. They are already
into debate strategy.

Debate can be a method of problem solving for Americans if
conducted for that purpose. But for me that is only one of the
gains. Debate can be a way of motivating people to work harder

for a mutually shared goal, of implanting a sense of togetherness among corporate trainees, of "energizing" their hidden drive as well as their knowledge, and of awakening them into articulation of their own individual identity.

In other words, with a touch of *hara*-logical approach in my debate and negotiation seminars, trainees and trainers become one. It is only through getting into each other's *hara* that the difference between the teachers and the taught disappears and we as one can have it both ways: mind-logic and *hara*-logic.

E. Japanese myth and legend made *haragei* feminine.

According to Japanese mythology, in the beginning was chaos, compared to floating oil, or to an egg without form, but containing the germs of life. The amorphous nature of Japanese *wa* is similar to the chaos. Amaterasu Omikami, the Sun Goddess, played the role of the central body, exercising both political and religious authority. The Goddess, the vague and symbolic character of the Yamato clan, ruled over Japan with the spirit of compromise and *wa* solution to conflict. The maintenance of *wa*, and avoidance of conflict, between or among heads of any clans or *ie* (family) has been the unwritten rule since mythological times. Japan's creation myth appears similar to the Vedic Concept of Creation.

> In the beginning was Hiranyagarbha (Golden Womb)
> The seed of elemental existence,
> The only Lord of all that was born.
> He upheld the heaven and earth together
> To what God other than Him,
> could we dedicate our life?   (Atharva 4.2.7)

But a closer look at the above verse unveils to us a clear distinction between a She-culture and a He-culture, despite the similarity in the very beginning. The ancient Aryan philosophers defined *asat* (non-being) as one only without second, from which proceeds the state of being. It did not require Him already born out of a divine womb to develop womb-like *hara* to be subtle, subservient or circumspect, a quality required of any Japanese leader worth his *hara*.

Japan is a Goddess culture. The leadership quality, such as decisiveness, courage, or strategic clarity, takes on a feminine tone. *Wa*—preservation within family—is one such leadership attribute. One speculates that it must have taken the Sun Goddess' *hara* to preserve the *wa* of the Divine Family. When Amaterasu sent her grandson, Ninigi, to become the ruler of the Central Land of Reed Plains, she gave him three treasures (*sanshu-no-jingi*) as a sign of his charge: a jeweled necklace (symbolizing benevolence), a mirror (purity), and the Herb-Quelling Sword (courage).

It would not be hard to infer, from the fact that *hara* happens to represent the above three basic human qualities, namely, benevolence, purity, and courage, that *hara* must have been employed as a symbolic gesture to keep the family together by putting God's fear of *wa* on the Divine Family members. The family still remains the basic unit of Japanese society. The village is the extension of the family.

In the premodern period, the extended family functioned as an economic unit based on its members' total obedience within a hierarchical structure. *Wa* among the villages, of which families are part, must be rigidly maintained. The principle of *wa*, as the family code, can be applied for corporate families and, by extension, for business communities (*zaikai*). Bureaucrats (*kankai*) use the subtle, swift sword called administrative guidance (*gyosei shido*) to make sure every business community preserves the rule of *wa*. Political parties (*seikai*) depend on the business communities for political donations to keep their houses in order in the spirit of *wa*, which, in turn, keep a close watch on bureaucrats (*kankai*) with a carrot and stick so that they behave according to the spirit of *wa*.

The three villages (*zaikai, seikai,* and *kankai*) are playing a three-person game of *wa* (sansukumi) in the form of a paper-scissors-rock game so that *wa* is maintained in a circular fashion for the entire country of Japan as in Figure 6.

Figure 6   A paper-scissors-rock game of wa played by the Japanese nation.

It is obvious that Japan has inherited a conventional wisdom of rice-growers since mythological times. Anyone (or any organization, for that matter) who destroys wa by rocking the boat is slowly thrown out of the circle by means of murahachibu (close to ostracization), like beans thrown out at the Setsubun's bean-throwing ceremony, with the remaining members chanting: "In with luck; out with the devil." Perhaps the most conclusive evidence to support the claim that wa is impregnable can be found even in the behavior of yakuza (violent antisocial groups), which is characterized by: (1) loyalty to the oyabun (boss) or ikka (family), (2) hierarchical orientation, (3) ritual expression of humility, (4) sensitivity to kao (face), (5) intergroup courtesy and exclusion, and (6) body symbolism, including tattooing. Foreign observers wonder how much the yakuza family differs from the corporate family (or the political family) since members of both even today remain ready to lay their lives on the line (*karada-o-haru*) for the sake of *wa*. Confrontations between private *wa*-seekers can resolve themselves in nebulous *haragei*.

IV

HOW DOES *HARAGEI* WORK IN JAPAN?
—A Breathing Game—

A. *Haragei* is all breathing

1. Clean *haragei* and dirty *haragei*

In ancient times, the moment when both sumo wrestlers were holding their breaths was called "*aiki-no-ma*" (moment of psychic agreement), which is crucial in successful *tachiai* (the point when the fight begins) in sumo. Since timing at *tachiai* (encounter) is considered the moment of truth in a sumo game, the synchronization of breathing calls for repeated *shikirinaoshi* (gestures of combat-readiness). The spring labor struggle (*shunto*) in this light is exactly a non-physical sumo between management and labor, through *shikirinaoshi* rituals which are repeated for month after month in the form of symbolic protests like threatening strikes. And strangely, their breaths meet somewhere along the line. Back to the original circle.

In this ritual game of *shunto*, no game-playing lawyers or labor consultants can hope to obtain an everybody-wins solution (*enman kaiketsu*) unless they perform *haragei* to bring about the synchronization of breathing as the sumo *gyoji* (referee) does. *Haragei* masters, experts in intuition-action, perceive others' breathing and make an instant decision to get on or off their breathlength. One of the parties may have already made up his *hara (hara o kimeru)*. However, because of the absence of visible or audible messages exchanged, the decision may not be confirmed by the outsiders. The truth remains unclear. So what? Breathing is the name of the game in Japan, in *omiai*, sumo wrestling, or *shunto* (the spring labor offensive).

What debate is to boxing, *haragei* is to sumo. The abundance of sumo jargon in our daily conversation is its proof: *gappuri yottsu ni kumi* (literally, mutual grapping, without clinching and therefore admirable), *ucchari* and *hatakikomi* (both sneaky and unaesthetic). The essence of sumo is breathing. Breathing is what brings out the truth. In Hinduism, *atman* (Sanskrit for breath) means a principle of life, spirit, or soul. The etymological parallel for *atman* is the Greek *psyche*, meaning breath, life, and soul. Mutual breathing is a key to successful *haragei* as in sumo's *tachiai*. However, the successful coming together in the middle of the ring would be impossible without the promoter of mutual breathing, called *gyoji*, a master of ceremonies resembling a referee. The *gyoji's* job is to bring the opponents onto the same breathlength through the symbolic gesture of saying *"Miatte"* ("Look each other in the eyes").

The long ceremonial *shikirinaoshi* prior to the actual clash is considered by sumo buffs to be even more important than the brief moment of physical contact. Besides being a time of tension build-up for spectators, it is also a time for psychological measuring up of one's opponent through studying the opponent's breathing and psyching oneself up before *tachiai*.

Foreign businessmen tend to ignore the breathing aspect of Japanese culture built into the tradition-bound Japanese system. Nothing could be more disturbing to the Japanese businessmen than having their breath taken away by the Western businessmen's rapid-fire questions, ignoring a breath-identification part of communication: "You said, 'Wait.' But how much time do we have to wait?" "Why?" "You've been saying 'wait' since we first met each other."

Psycho-tactics play a part in sumo. When the wrestlers fail to breathe together, one or both will indicate unreadiness for combat (*matta o kakeru*), whereupon the *gyoji* gives them another chance to synchronize their breathing. A clever sumo wrestler may use a *matta* tactic of "Wait! I'm not ready," to deliberately disturb his opponent's breathing. This is not very clean. The mind play may win the short-term game but to win long-term trust *hara* action is a must. Boxers' approach of attempted "psychs" does not work in Japan. Baseball players' "psych" game of bench-jockeying and knock-down pitches does not work either in Japan. Nor do the footballers' intimidation tactics. Do not "psych" others out. *Haragei* is no chess game. The guy with the killer instinct will be the first to get outside the circle of the sumo ring.

Haragei, being essentially a breathing game, comes in two types: clean *haragei* and dirty *haragei*. The criterion for determining cleanliness in *haragei* acting lies in naturalness of breathing. When breathing becomes quick and shallow, thought processes get disorderly . . . and it all shows.

The point is to be natural and effortless through breath control. This does not mean being yourself; it means being inside your opponent through "breath transference," thus acting naturally and contextually. Too great an effort to play one's cards close to the chest is poor tactics; it will not do to have one's motives unjustly suspected. Verbal sparring is more or less taboo in Japan, hence catching each other's breathing is the key to successful interpersonal communication and perhaps crosscultural communication as well.

Haragei masters are invariably deep breathers. They are quick to detect changes in breathing since they know that while conscious verbalizing can be deceptive, unconscious breathing is not. They may not be smooth talkers. But they are capable of listening to their partner's wordy silence and then may either join him in his breathing or let him join in theirs by means of well-timed *ma* or pregnant pauses. Carrying this analogy into the more immediate corporate life, intra- or inter-office *nemawashi* can be considered the counterpart of this building-up *shikirinaoshi* period in sumo.

2. Breathing rules for would-be *haragei* practitioners

To practice *haragei*, you must learn to breathe correctly. To breathe correctly means to breathe contextually, because the context has built-in relativity: yang and yin, or what Spinoza called *natura naturans* (the active and vital process) and *natura naturata* (the passive product). If the two were translated into English, a linear language, they would be substance and mode or essence and incident. Obviously the translation is misleading. But accepting the linear translation of the circular notion of yang and yin, the circular *haragei* can be linearly decomposed: *hara* as essence and *gei* (art) as incident. Then it follows from this that *haragei* corresponds to breathing, because breathing is the essence of life and art is definitely the incident of breathing.

Breathing has two aspects: inhale and exhale. While a karate fighter attacks on the exhale and defends on the inhale, the *haragei* master simply times his breathing and decides contextually whether or not to keep his mouth closed or open. Westerners who grow up with faith in symmetrical interpersonal relationships tend to feel perplexed when suddenly exposed to the asymmetrical situation in Japan. Seeing that women, except bar hostesses, usually remain silent and unobtrusive behind attention-getting males, they conclude that the male-female relationship is unbalanced. Wrong. Look at the guardian sculptures in front of a Shinto shrine and you will notice one of the two Korean dogs has his mouth open and the other closed. They personify *a* (yang) and *un* (yin), active and passive—a perfect breathing relationship called in Japan *a-un-no-kokyu*. In *haragei*, an art of well-timed breathing, obtaining exhaler-inhaler rapport (*a-un-no-kokyu*) remains its highest form.

Haragei masters-to-be, first and foremost, must learn the art of breathing. Here are the nine rules of standard breathing procedures that must be observed to qualify as a *haragei* practitioner.

1. Breathing must be deep. There are four types of breathing: with the shoulders, the chest, the *hara* (abdomen), and the toes. Deep breathing here means with the *hara*.

2. Breathing must be quiet.
3. Breathing must be long. You must learn to take as long a breath as possible.
4. Breathing must be steadily rhythmical. It must follow the rhythmic and repetitive pattern of exhaling-stop-inhaling-stop and back to exhaling.
5. Holding your breath is as important as breathing itself, since it signifies *ma*, a breathing pause.
6. Breathing must be done with the correct posture. You must keep your spine as straight as possible but not tense.
7. Breathing must be performed to create energy. The energy created by breathing is called *prana* in yoga and *chi* in Taoism. Breathing, according to Shinto, purifies stains in your mind or *hara*.
8. Breathing must be done unconsciously. You must learn to get control of the rhythm of breathing until breathing becomes part of you.
9. Breathing must be done to discover yourself in the midst of nature. You must be able to develop your cosmic consciousness or identify with the mother earth through nirvana-seeking breaths.

B. Psychological preparedness to enter *haragei*

Ruth Benedict, author of a widely-read book in Japan, *The Chrysanthemum and the Sword*, contemplates the Japanese nature with this observation: "The Japanese are, to the highest degree, both aggressive and unaggressive, both militaristic and aesthetic, both insolent and polite, rigid and adaptable, submissive and resentful of being pushed around, loyal and treacherous, brave and timid, conservative and hospitable to new ways. They are terribly concerned about what other people will think of their behavior, and they are also overcome by guilt when other people know nothing of their misstep. Their soldiers are disciplined to the hilt but also insubordinate." (pages 2–3)

Ruth Benedict's observations of the Japanese, viewed from without, are illogical. However, if the Japanese are observed from within, they are simply *hara*-logical. The mind-logical Westerners tend to say "no" when they mean "no" or gamely say "yes" when they mean "no." The *hara*-logical Japanese accepts either "yes" or "no" as it comes, and rejects nothing. *Hara*-logic and *haragei* truth are in a category of their own.

Accepting a thing as it is (*aru-ga-mama*) or as it comes (*shizen-no-mama*) is part of the nature of *haragei*. The main tenet of Morita's therapeutic philosophy is accepting things "as they are." Their "let nature take its course" slogan is an exercise of *hara*-logic. Patients following the philosophy must "stomach," or unite with, their sufferings and worries just as they are, and must "cut open their *hara*" (*hara-o-waru*) without relying on their rationality as therapeutic leverage. To resolve the conflict between "yes" and "no," one must first forget about logic and learn to communicate by *hara*-logic.

1. Say No at your own risk.

If debate is an efficient means of solving problems, *haragei* is an effective means of "internalizing" and "neutralizing" them. Debate can be suicidal in Japan, because it means an unaesthetic conflict of opinion, which runs contrary to the indigenous value of *wa* (intra-group harmony or nonconfrontation), and running a risk of causing others to lose face. To refute someone's opinion often means to attack the person personally, which, in turn, means an eventual falling out. Particularly in politics, where *haragei* is a standard operating procedure, the truth not only hurts but can make one bleed to death. A case in point is the purge from the Japan Communist Party of Satomi Hakamada, its vice-chairman. Why was he expelled? Part of the reason can be found in his reply to an interviewer with the *Japan Times*: "May we interpret what you have said in the following way? On the wording of 'Dictatorship of the proletariat,' on China's nuclear weapons tests, and on the JCP's policies toward China and the Soviet Union, you did not have great differences with the Miyamoto leadership. But you had critical differences on how to create a mass movement and a labor movement." "Yes, that was the decisive factor." (*Japan Times*, February 8, 1978)

Thus the expulsion resulted from a conflict of opinion. JCP Chairman Miyamoto said in effect, "*Akahata* readers will help in carrying out a Communist revolution. So increase them to 5 million," whereas Hakamada said in essence, "No. *Akahata* readers are just subscribers. We should not depend on them so much for the revolution." They touched base on the goal of revolution, but the means to achieve it was mutually unacceptable. Result: expulsion. Surely American readers, who have grown up watching on television such controversy programs as The Last Word, Nightline, Phil Donahue, and The People's Court, will justifiably wonder how a mere difference of opinion could lead to the expulsion of a longtime comrade from the Party? But such a thought hardly occurs to the average *haragei* practitioner who freezes to hear Barbara Walters' questions in her interview program, because the Japanese know that a conflict of opinion often develops into a conflict of personality.

Haragei masters would say that the two men should have avoided such a counter-productive confrontation by using *haragei*. And Miyamoto allegedly did warn Hakamada with a *haragei* message: "Comrade Hakamada, please don't state your opinions at meetings. If you have anything to say, please say it to me directly," meaning privately. Although Miyamoto later publicly denied this, his *hara*-message was obvious: To embarrass me in public means your political suicide; therefore don't contradict me in public. Use *haragei* for everlasting friendship or "enemyship"— both are correct in the *haragei* lexicon. If *haragei* had worked between them, the internal struggle might have been kept private. Once the private problem area becomes public, more intense, life-or-death *haragei* acting has to be performed to mend the broken emotional fence. The historic non-verbal *haragei* negotiation between Katsu Kaishu and Saigo Takamori is a classic example of how *haragei* can be effectively employed to mend a fence broken almost beyond repair.

Once I went so far as to try and have a debate in English with a professor of a prestigious university in Japan on whether or not English is spoken logic (my belief), after the professor had criticized in the magazine *English Education* the argument which I developed in my book *Give and Get* (Asahi Press). I wrote a rejoinder in the same magazine and privately asked the chief editor of the magazine to make an arrangement for an open debate between the professor and myself with native speakers as judges. I was insensitive. His reply: "A very good idea. But I recommend you sit on the *tatami* with him and adjust the differences privately, *never* openly. Privately you can say no and compromise, but publicly you cannot say no without compromising your principle or your political life." No productive dialogue ensued afterwards. The moral: Use *haragei* to say no and to retain privacy.

The *haragei* mentality can be compared with the structure of the rooms of a Japanese house. Open the sliding doors (*fusuma*) of each and every room and you will see the whole house as one room. "Sitting on the *tatami* knee to knee" is a more congenial way of adjusting differences than sitting across the negotiating table eyeball to eyeball. Choose tatami for *haragei* because the intimate feeling of *tatami* helps minimize the difference between yes and no.

Back to the JCP's in-fighting, what might have happened if Hakamada and Miyamoto had chosen to sit on the *tatami* to keep their differences private? There would have been no acrimonious exchange of public charges and countercharges which even touched on the question of who was responsible in the ancient 1933 police-informer "murder" case. So yesterday's sworn friends literally became today's sworn enemies. This seems to have lead some foreign observers to believe erroneously that they cannot make real friends with Japanese people because friendship as they know it in Japan is temporary and situational—therefore, undependable. Wrong. *Haragei* practitioners are more relativistic and tolerant in their thinking. They would say, "Yesterday's enemies can turn out to be today's friends; after all, enemy and friend are one and the same. The worst crime is to put people into two categories: friends and enemies, citizens and criminals."

Perhaps a clearer perspective can be gained by contrasting the traditional nonconfrontational Japanese friend-enemy relationship with the traditionally adversary Western angel-devil cosmography. The man of *haragei* regards an associate as neither friend nor enemy, and skillfully avoids taking sides or making value judgements, lest he commit social suicide by making a moral judgement. The absence of any really bloody conflict between the Chrysanthemum (the Imperial family) and the Sword (the shogunate, or government), and the unbroken Imperial line in Japan's recorded history, are proof of the success of the long-standing *haragei*-guided nonconfrontational confrontation—hobnobbing between the government (which rules) and the Emperor (who reigns).

The suave *haragei* performer avoids taking sides in public by using vague or neutral phases pregnant with hidden messages. If someone as a feeler drops the name of a wheeler-dealer (*yarite*) whom I don't happen to like, I do not say, "I hate his guts," or, "Put me in touch with him because I'm interested in him." Instead, I probably say in a detached manner with a slightly lowered tone of voice, "He's a very *kiyoona-hito*." The tone is slightly negative, but I have avoided any future personality conflict resulting from my taking sides. Or I might say, "He sounds interesting . . ." implying, "If your description of him is adequate," thus diversifying the risk of taking sides.

This adjective, *kiyoona*, means a combination of an offputtingly shrewd, time-serving, back-slapping, table-hopping, glad-hander type and an attractively clever, suave, sensitive survivor.

A noncommittal hint is not considered bad taste in Japan, but a sign of sophistication. I often hear complaints of Japanese English being too ambiguous, using maybe, perhaps, yes-but, and other semi-verbal stop-gap phrases and pauses, revealing an effort to avoid saying no in public. James Levine, opera conductor with the Metropolitan Opera House, is clever at avoiding comments on his colleagues' performances for fear of being pinned down about his favorite pieces of music. But if he uses the above weapon of vague language, he does not have to take sides or get trapped either way. Conductors and *haragei* practitioners have a lot in common—demonstrated strength in a balancing act. Conductors don't play any specific musical instrument, they play the orchestra. *Haragei* masters don't dance with individuals. They let others dance to the music of the orchestra they play.

2. Japanese No's

An American observer may jokingly comment on the Japanese language: "There is no Japanese equivalent of the English 'no.' There is only Noooooo . . . in Japan." But *haragei* masters counter the argument by saying, "If 'no' means 'no' and the 'no' is directly and unaesthetically employed, *haragei*, an art of saying 'no' without saying 'no' and saying 'yes' without saying 'yes,' will lose its beauty." These twenty rules to avoid saying 'no' will give you some insights into how *hara*-logical Japanese say 'no' in substance.

I. Don't answer. If you are not willing to answer any question—for example, during cross-examination—a long *ssaaa* well suffice. In ordinary conversations, you might as well keep breaking your listener's silence by constantly saying "yes, yes, yes," to show you are listening with interest, but don't show willingness to commit yourself to saying "yes" or "no" to any meaningful questions. Keeping on nodding vertically (not necessarily affirmatively) without answering works too. Or just say, "Ummm." If the person twists your arm, say politely, "I'll leave it to your imagination." Or drop your eyes and don't look up. Better still, do not listen.

"What is your personal opinion about dumping?"

"We have been sincere." "Or about violation of COCOM regulations?"

"We have been sincere."

II. Keep the other person hanging with vague answers. The surefire way to cause the other person to lose face is to give him a flat no. Therefore, the best way to keep the person at arm's length is to keep him or her hanging by giving vague answers, such as "maybe" or "perhaps."

> "I want to make an announcement tonight that I'm going to get married to you."

"Please wait."

"Why?"

"Because I said please wait."

"Does that mean no?"

"Maybe."

"It also means yes, doesn't it?"

"Maybe."

III. Be extremely polite.   Make the other person feel too comfortable to bother to ask you if your gesture means "yes" or "no." Excessive politeness usually means "no." Kyoto-born *haragei* doers make a practice of politely insisting that a guest take a cup of tea before leaving while expecting you to refuse it. To take it means one is a *nangi-na-hito* (an insensitive person). Yuji Aida, former professor of Kyoto University, claims: "To be extremly polite to your guest is the most imaginative way to get him out of your house." By the same token, you could keep on saying in a broken-record fashion: "I absolutely agree with you" or "I can't agree with you more." And never give him or her the time of day. A member of the Liberal Democratic Party once told me of *haragei*: "It means: the higher the rank of the politician climbs, the lower his posture gets. The best way to resolve the conflict or infighting is to keep your head down. The more powerful persons must be more polite and ready to apologize first to the less powerful in Japan. This is how *haragei* works in politics."

IV. Give the other person the situation, and not the reason.   To avoid falling into the trap of giving a "no" answer, one might as well give a situation instead of a reason. Examples: 1) "Why did you marry that foolish, ugly, disobedient woman?" "That's beside the point. The fact is I'm already married. *Shikataganai* (undebatable), isn't it? We must say good-bye to each other." "Why?" "I love you, but . . ." "But why?" "Uh . . . the situation doesn't permit us to stay in love. You know it. *Shikataganai.*" 2) "Why is the quality of the Japanese products so high?" "Because it's Sony." "Why can't General Electric make their quality higher?" "Because, well, eh, it's Japanese." "Does that mean American brains are inferior?" "I don't mean that. Because I think our brains are unique."

V. Inflate the other person's ego while deflating yours.   If a woman doesn't want to marry you, she can give you a polite run-around by saying, "You deserve more than a woman of my looks, brain, and social status can offer." Another example: "Japan is not No. 1, it's No. 51. Look at the statistics. Crime. Education. Etc, etc, etc . . ." "Yes, as a Japanese, I agree with you one hundred percent." "What?" "So please tell it to the government of Japan."

VI. Deliberately get off the central issue.   Westerners often complain that in any verbal conflict the Japanese tend to deviate from the central issue and instead react to their reaction or take it personally. Examples: 1) "Why do you kill dolphins so mercilessly?" "You'll never understand the unique nature of the Japanese culture." 2) "Before answering that question, let me talk about . . ." 3) "I don't like the way you talk." 4) "Not to change the subject . . ." 5) "Mr. Wakanohana, how do you feel about the loss of your son?" "Do you have a son?" 6) "This is what I believe." "You say so, because you are young."

VII. Use vague language.   In one scene of Kurosawa's *The Bad Sleep Well,* Kuromaku (a behind-the-scenes *haragei* bigwig) said to his aide: "Get him in a car and drop him there." The aide said: "Why?" The *hara-no-kuroi* (scheming) politician, a little angry, blurted out: "*Bokuni-iwaseruno-kane*?" The superimposed translation is "Must I say it?" But this translation is too direct. My word-for-word translation, without losing the original flavor of the meaning, is more subtle and indirect: "Do you want to let me say it?" Further translation: "Kill him. But I didn't say it. Okay?" Another example: "If I think I'm satisfied, I'm satisfied; if I think I'm not satisfied, I'm not satisfied."

VIII. Make your argument abstract and metaphysical.   Don't argue about the specific issue, but develop your argument philosophically. In other words, be less specific and less concrete. An example: "Prime Minister, what are you trying to accomplish during this tour of ASEAN nations?" "To develop heart-to-heart contact. It also means mind-to-mind. My mind is as clear as the moon reflected on the surface of a pond (a Zen quotation)." Your questioner will almost surely get lost if he or she is logical.

IX. *Pass the buck to the "air."*   In the close-knit Japanese system where the responsibility is shared among members for any action taken for the attainment of a commonly-shared goal, the buck stops nowhere as it often turns out. Any group develops its own peculiar ethos or *kuki* (air), and a member can hide behind *tatemae* (group-self). Example: "Why did you agree then?" "How could I possibly have said no under such *kuki* (atomospherics)?" (meaning, I told a *tatemae* truth, but not a *honne* truth). This art of buckpassing to the impersonal "air" is a more sophisticated way of getting around the situation than singling out a buckpassee. However, it may help save your skin or face, but you will lose your *hara*, which will prove more costly in the long run.

X. *Pity yourself.*   *Haragei* users are skillful negotiators from a position of weakness. Crying wolf is also an effective means of waiting and fighting back at the right moment. "*Yowatta.*" ("I'm in trouble" is the word-for-word translation, but the cultural translation is "No.") "*Sonna koto iwaretemo komarimasu wa.*" ("To say such a thing will put me on the spot.") "*Muzukashii ne.*" ("It's difficult.") Translation of the above three in most cases: Over my dead body, you will.

XI. *Generalize a particular matter.*   Foreigners often feel uncomfortable to hear the Japanese say, "*We* Japanese think such and such." *Haragei* practitioners, as well as most Japanese, assume that what they feel is what others feel. "What is your opinion about living together?" "Generally speaking . . ." "No, I'm asking you." "Publicly speaking . . . , privately speaking . . ." "Which is *your* opinion?" "Generally speaking, a public man like me thinks . . ."

XII. *Keep them guessing.*   Psychologist Hiroshi Ishikawa, a professor at Seijo University, states in his book *How to Say No Without Saying No*: "The politician's primary tactic is frequently to use catch-all terms that can be interpreted differently by each person.

If his listeners interpret it as "no," there's no problem. If it is interpreted as "yes," he can also get away with it by saying, "I didn't say 'yes.'" You can state your own opinion on another person without saying you don't like him: "Why don't people like him? He's a nice guy." Translation: I don't like him either.

XIII.· Be sure to say "yes" first and add "but" later. The yes-but tactic isn't a unique Japanese phenomenon. What is so unique about the Japanese yes-but syndrome is that it is the norm here in Japan. "I think your theory makes a lot of sense but . . . (negative)" "Yes, that's what the law says, but . . . (negative)" "Maybe I'm wrong, but . . . (You're wrong)" etc. Here's a universally useful yes-but tactic, yet a bit un-Japanese. "Yes, I would very much like to contribute an article to your weekly magazine for housewives. But I hope you will give me a chance next time to write a lengthy article on either cyrogenics and earth-worms, or bloodtypes and temperaments of wild monkeys." This would be the last tactic I would use against the disagreeable publisher. But luckily I have never met a publisher I did not like.

The feudal lord, Tadaoki Hosokawa, known as a man of *hara*, once had to render justice to two *samurai* caught in the act of homosexuality, which was strictly forbidden and punishable by *seppuku*. Seeing determination on the faces of the two convicted men to accept death, if so sentenced, Tadaoki Hosokawa said solemnly, "How courageous of you to engage in a forbidden act of homosexuality, risking *harakiri*. No doubt, you would prove yourself genuine soldiers on the battle ground. I'll grant you a pardon. And don't break up." And to the greater surprise of his stunned entourage not only did the Lord judge them not guilty but also gave rewards to the two gay *samurai*. But since he put the two *samurai* out to pasture after having stripped them of titles, the two began to fall out with each other and thereafter went straight.

XIV. Make someone a sacrificial lamb. To maintain a harmonious whole in a consensus society such as Japan's, protruding corners must be cut off. This has to be done subtly and ceremoniously in accordance with time-honored customs. The ceremonial way of dealing with non-conformists can be observed in everyday situations. An example: A *haragei*-practicing boss might casually say to you and your friends: "Mr. Tanaka is lazy because he leaves his office at five o'clock sharp." An employee who does not understand *haragei* interprets this to mean that his boss doesn't like Tanaka and grins from ear to ear triumphantly. A *haragei*-practicing employee interprets this as a covert warning not to leave his office at five, lest he be regarded as a lazy person by others. "To unkill two birds with one stone . . ." This is a common tactic employed by a man of small *hara*. A man of bigger *hara* never makes a sacrificial lamb of a single person. He admires his men behind their backs: "Tanaka gets credit from management, because he never leaves the office till he gets his job done." The message: The listener must work harder to get his boss's approval.

XV. Use a group decision to give a negative answer. You may often hear a Japanese say, "I wish I could help you, but the group doesn't permit me to." To insist he persuade the group would be considered *yabo* or insensitive because his answer, even when he is in an influential position within the company, is "no." This blame-the-group tactic works in a society where the buck moves in a circle. This fits in with the traditional culture of Japan where people are encouraged to grow up as group-thinkers rather than individual thinkers. Decline by solemnly saying, "We have had a series of discussions, and we are sorry to inform you that . . ."

XVI. Get an outsider to say 'no' for you. It's morally, ethically, and aesthetically difficult for the Japanese to say 'no' directly. However, since the *haragei* axiom is "Saying 'no' *directly* hurts people," it is by no means immoral, unethical, or unaesthetic to get an outsider as a buffer zone to do the job for you. Of course, the best person for the job is a *haragei* master. The last person for the job: a lawyer. The history of Japan bears out the fact that Japan has had to rely on foreign pressure to change the domestic system. To get cheaper beef, Japanese consumers must depend on American pressure. Writing an expose of racial discrimination in Japan is considered a taboo among Japanese journalists. Strangely (justifiably, by *hara*-logic), non-Japanese seem to be able to get away with it. Why not give the nasty job to them?

XVII. Get tough when cornered.   Assume a "So what?" attitude when cornered, or threaten to do *sashichigae*, or force upon your enemy a mutual suicide (by stabbing each other). "Yes, I did the wrong thing. But so what? I did it for the sake of my company." Or: "If you do that, I'll do *sashichigae* with you or involve you in *shinju* (double suicide)." *Sashichigae* smacks of "forced double suicide" and the mere mention of it is enough to make the listener shudder. The employees of Nissho-Iwai (a general trading company) must have shuddered to hear Kaifu, an executive and wheeler-dealer in the corporation, say publicly on a political scandal case over the Grumman deal, "I'll do *sashichigae* (mutual stabbing) with Ueda (the chairman)."

XVIII. Blame your place or role for forcing you to say 'no.'   Everyone in Japan is *bun*-conscious. The anthropological and sociological *bun* means "status to be occupied and role to be carried out." Both status and role are relational concepts because they exist in relation to another status or role. And they can be employed to say "no." Examples: 1) "I wish I could help you. But unfortunately, I'm not in the right position or in the right role to do so." 2) "I agree with you completely, but being an employee of the ministry concerned, I can't say 'yes.'"

XIX. Blame en.   *En* is something predetermined in a previous life. How can one change it unilaterally? One of the best ways to say "good-bye" without hurting the feelings of your friend is to blame *en*. Say "No *en*," or "There was no *en* from the beginning," and the other party will soon get the message: "She doesn't like me any more. You can't blame Cupid. *Shikataganai*."

XX. Play dumb.   The Japanese, contrary to popular belief, do have a sense of humor. Their jokes, often depending on plays on words (*share* or puns), are likely to be discredited by the linear-minded Westerners as of a low standard. But an imaginative play on words can be extremely helpful in softening the highly charged atmosphere. The *haragei* master's weapon of *toboke* (playing dumb) is an extension of play on words. Examples: "What is the name of the bird, interpreter?" "Ask the bird." "Prime Minister Sato, what is the Japanese attitude regarding foreign aid to developing nations." "Ask Secretary General U. Thant of the United Nations." "Prime Minister Ohira, could you address yourself to the whaling issue?" "The whale is too big an animal for me." "Minister Sakurauchi, do you think the problem of trade friction between Japan and the United States will go away?" "My name is cherry (*sakura*). It will go away beautifully."

C. *Haragei* in action

1. How *nemawashi* works in Japan

Nemawashi: "The act of digging around the root of a big tree one or two years before its scheduled transplantation, and clipping off all but the main root and the large branch-roots and allowing new root hairs to grow, thus facilitating the transplantation, and also enabling the tree to bear better fruit."—*Kojien* dictionary

When Katsu Kaishu, representing the crumbling Tokugawa Shogunate, and Saigo Takamori, representing the Imperial forces trying to take over Edo Castle, held their historic final negotiation in 1868, both parties employed *haragei*. But it was because of Katsu's *nemawashi* that the bloodless surrender of Edo Castle to the Imperial forces could be negotiated through *haragei* between the two. Katsu, besides having obtained a budget of considerable size from the Shogun's coffers through *nemawashi*, made the *nemawashi* rounds almost every day to a phalanx of volunteer firefighter organizations and local bosses and also assembled them at meetings in his mansion as part of his unique crisis management. He also gathered fishermen on the coast to discuss an exodus in the event of failure in the negotiations. Katsu had been determined to set the town on fire should attacks be made by Saigo following the breakdown in the historic *hara*-to-*hara* confrontation. His *hara* enlarged through these friendly *nemawashi* gestures and incessant information-gathering efforts behind the scenes. Katsu's *hara* matched that of Saigo, a gutsy hero of proven *hara*. When the two archrivals met in a room of the Satsuma mansion in Tokyo, there was no exchange of explosive words but fiery give-and-take of implosive *hara* between them. Katsu's *hara* communicated to Saigo's. The taciturn Saigo slapped his thigh and tacitly agreed to accept Katsu's offer. *Nemawashi* saved Tokyo from a disaster, because *nemawashi* made *haragei* work. The lesson of this historic event lives on today even in the business world.

Particularly noticeable is the test of *hara* during the ritualistic confrontation of *shunto* (the spring labor offensive), when top intuitive leaders with analytical skills from a central labor committee and from management must, through the breathing game, assess each other's *hara*. They must also assess the mood surrounding the negotiations, relative bargaining power, the ability of the union to endure a long strike, infighting within the union, and the merits and demerits of a prolonged strike against the possible losses and gains. Far more crucial than the climax of the *haragei* showdown above is the *nemawashi* as explained by Taishiro Shirai:

"Since decisions of the legislative councils are by consensus or majority vote, the top leaders must engage in various political maneuvers to obtain majority support. The executive officers are weak in statutory rights and duties, and decisions are made collectively; hence it is essential that the officers retain the support of their trusted factions and caucuses. If the leader's faction does not command a stable majority, he must negotiate with other factions, even those in overt opposition, in order to move the convention in the desired direction. Hence, *nemawashi* is carried out prior to the formal debate and vote. In many cases, the formal decision on the floor is little more than a ceremony to confirm the decision already reached behind closed doors. In such cases, decision-making is done in places and through procedures totally unknown to the rank-and-file union member. Great ability or wisdom in such political maneuvers is one of the most important qualities of a union leader."

Let me give you a plausible context in which *nemawashi* works in Japan. In a certain company one day, a division manager, Geihara, told one of his subordinates, "I am being demoted to our subsidiary. I'm not being fired, so there's a chance that I'll come back with a higher position. How about coming with me to the subsidiary?" Hearing this, Jokawa trembled with fear because he had suddenly heard something totally unexpected from his superior for whom he had great affection. He replied, "I have great trust in you and would like to go anywhere with you. However, I don't think I am capable enough..." The division manager laughed and said, "Never mind. It's not that important."

Chitani, the second subordinate to hear the same thing from the division manager, replied, "This is rather sudden. Will you give me three days to think it over?" Chitani then did some thorough research on why he was approached, why division manager Geihara was demoted, whether the subsidiary had any future possibilities, and if he would profit from playing loyal to Geihara. He learned that an MITI official was coming into the company as a director in charge of Geihara's division. Because Geihara was a man of *hara*, and reputed to have what it takes to be a big-time boss, the company's board of directors felt that he would handle the MITI man easily.

A tacit agreement had been made, Chitani found out, between the directors and Geihara himself that in the future, Geihara would return triumphantly to the parent company after falling out with the former MITI official over a disagreement, while giving the parachuted official yet another parachute further down. After that, business as usual. "So that's why the division manager asked me to go with him," Chitani thought to himself and chuckled. He told division manager Geihara with enthusiasm, "Sir, I shall go with you," and bowed his head. The division manager's reaction was cool, "No need for you to come with me anymore."

After having talked to the first two, Geihara had approached a third subordinate, Haraishi, a samurai type. It takes a samurai employee of *hara* to identify with his samurai boss of *hara*. The samurai dedication exemplified by Haraishi's reaction to corporate life is a key to the success of Japanese business. Haraishi is a listener, not a talker; a reacter not an acter. While he is listening he focuses on his *hara*. He does not interrupt the speaker for further clarification and simply lets the speaker talk it out. He listens with his *hara* and it is in his *hara* that all the thoughts and possible conclusions are neutralized. Haraishi listened hard, while nodding, "yes, yes," with virtually no expression on his face. His mind may have been resting, but his *hara* was busily functioning like a water fowl with its legs busily paddling under water in an attempt to come up with the right moment to say, "When, sir?"—never, "Why?"

After hearing what Geihara said for twenty minutes Haraishi gave a prompt answer: "With pleasure. I won't ask why." In talking to the three subordinates, Geihara had deliberately put himself in a bad light by saying, "I am being demoted." This was a *haragei* tactic used to probe others' *hara*.

Mr. Geihara's *hara* got through only to Haraishi. Geihara never gave an order. But as it turned out his men made individual decisions. How? Jokawa used his heart to make his decision. Chitani used his mind to make his decision. In contrast, Haraishi had his *hara* made up. . . . Haraishi was not hesitant to commit love suicide with his superior. A subtle form of collective consensus forming.

The mind changes easily, but *hara* does not. To amplify this point, let us take a further look at this man Haraishi.

Even in ordinary times, Haraishi had done some *nemawashi* with his wife. He had kept telling her, "The life of a salaried employee is wretched. He is like a pawn in chess. On the company's order he has to go anywhere in the world. I hope you will always be prepared to accept such an eventuality." The wife had said, "It can't be helped. After all, I am the wife of a salaried employee. I have told the children that they, too, must expect to transfer schools at any time."

She is a woman whose *hara* is firmly made up. What's more, she had not neglected to do her own *nemawashi* with the children.

Their family is like that of the samurai in the service of the feudal lord. It is partly this sense of loyalty of employees which keeps business corporations together in Japan.

Even today, evidence of employees induced by offers of doubled pay to switch companies is scanty. It is an indication that Japanese society still values the "samurai employee" who feels an emotional commitment to his company and sacrifices his personal interests for the good of the company.

But getting back to our story, we find that Mr. Geihara, who has confirmed Haraishi's innermost heart, breathes a sigh of relief. Next day, Geihara receives a phone call from the director in charge of his division, "Let's have a drink tonight." At the high-class Japanese restaurant, the director says, "I'm sure you must have heard rumors already; if you were ordered to switch immediately to our subsidiary, would you agree?"

"I'm ready anytime, sir." "Is that so? Are there any subordinates who will go with you?" "I've done the *nemawashi* already." "Boy, you're a fast operator, aren't you ? Here, have a drink." Geihara is as cool as a cucumber as he asks, "Sir, is this really going to happen?" "Well, to tell the truth, it seems that such a decision may be made by the board of directors soon. Actually, we still don't know much about the character of the official who is being sent by MITI to join our company."

"You mean that the decision has not yet been made?" "That's right. Ha, ha, ha. Your *hara* isn't big enough to see through my *hara*. Ha, ha, ha." This is a variation of *haragei* casually performed by businessmen worth their *hara*. Although the decision has not yet been made *nemawashi* is going on at all levels just to make sure that *haragei* is working. Thus, all the groundwork is completed to cope with the situation in case MITI does send an official into the company. Business as usual.

The following incident actually occurred. MITI ordered the dissolution of the Japan Commerce Promotion Association, a public service organization under MITI's jurisdiction, when it learned that the Association was operating a gold market which was outside the purpose for which the Association was formed.

Masatoshi Matsushita, the president of the Association, reacted angrily:

"The operation of a gold market may not be in line with our articles of association. However, it is not proper to abruptly order the dissolution of the Association without having given us guidance in advance on rectifying the situation."

The position taken by Matsushita is that he admits a breach of the law but asserts that an abrupt order makes things inconvenient. This could mean, "MITI could and should have had the decency to conduct *nemawashi* well in advance." It is difficult to discipline Japanese corporations by means of the law because, without fail, a nasty aftertaste lingers.

It is for this reason that the law is regarded in Japanese society as the "last resort" whose signficance lies in it not being invoked. *Gyosei shido*, administrative guidance, after all, is not law. *Gyosei shido* is something like air, and that is why it can be said that it is effective in Japan. This "air" takes many different forms—sometimes an instruction, sometimes a request, at other times a recommendation or even a warning—and acts as a pressure on business corporations.

If, for instance, MITI says to the president of a company, "Can you give a position in your company to one of our officials? He might not be so capable, but . . . By the way, we hear that your company has started futures transaction in gold . . . . Well, we won't go into that matter," the president cannot afford to ignore the casual remark. The president should feel grateful and say, "We welcome him." This is better for the company.

For MITI, the placing of an ex-official in a company means the establishment of a pipeline with that company. This traditional system, known as *amakudari* (literally, descending from heaven), works occasionally as a lubricant of two-way communication, if *nemawashi* is properly done.

There exists a mammoth disciplinary machinery which is even more feared than MITI. It is the Ministry of Finance. The *nemawashi* power of the Finance Ministry is so strong that it can even force the merger of commercial banks if it can be justified for reasons of effective financing. With the opening gambit of the Finance Ministry to get the financial world roped in through *nemawashi*, the mutual holding of shares between corporations, mergers, and even takeovers can become realities.

One of the major invisible barriers which make it impossible for Western corporations to take over Japanese companies is *nemawashi*. For instance, if a foreign corporation made a takeover bid of a Japanese company listed on the First Section of the Tokyo Stock Exchange, it would have to conduct *nemawashi* with, at least, both securities and banking bureaus of the Ministry of Finance, the Tokyo Stock Exchange, MITI, supporting banks and major stockholders of the company in question, political circles (through financial leaders), and the mass media. The psychological climate of Japan where nothing can be decided without *nemawashi* may be disturbing for American and European corporation managers who want quick action and relate it to the bottom line.

2. Why *nemawashi* is effective in Japan

There is a popular, conventional theory that Japan is a vertical society. Nothing could be more mistaken. Japan is a circular society. Japanese corporations, for instance, are the circular entities which, as I explained earlier, operate with both centripetal and centrifugal forces which are more forceful around the axis. In Japanese corporate structure, the common rule (exceptions exist) is the bottom-up method which is quite contrary to the top-down method in the Western corporate system. The circular *ringi* system (a group decision-making system) which is almost universal in major Japanese corporations, is the process of absorbing the ideas, determination, and commitment of those at the bottom and spiralling them up the echelons.

If Japanese society were really a pyramid-type vertical society, the *amakudari* with which it is identified would unfold in an entirely different manner. Everything would be settled with a single telephone call from MITI to the president of a company of a certain industry under MITI's jurisdiction: "We are going to send into your company an able man. Please take care of him." At a board meeting, the president would at once speak up:

"A MITI official will join our company day after tomorrow. Please make the necessary arrangements. Now, Suzuki, the new subsidiary is under your turf, isn't it? We'll get a pipeline into MITI, so you should be happy. Complete the new set-up in two or three days. Forget about the *ringi*. And forget about *nemawashi*. Get busy. Shape up or ship out."

Suzuki, the director in charge, would then get the department and section managers together and make a bombshell statement: "Listen, this is the official order. We must reorganize. . . . Here is my plan. . . . I shall now read out the names of those who will be given new assignments. Those named will immediately transfer their duties to others. Say 'no' at your own risk. That is all."

There is no room at all for *nemawashi* in this situation. What would be the consequences of such a process? Efficiency? But effectiveness?

1) The president would be regarded as dictatorial and the board directors would distrust him, leading to poor communication among top management.
2) A gulf would be created among individual directors and between the directors and middle management.
3) Management-labor relations would go sour.
4) The family atmosphere of the office would suddenly be chilly.
5) The sense of lost security would ripple over to the families of employees.
6) The official who came from MITI would be politely treated but not listened to by the directors of the new company.
7) The morale of the former MITI official would drop because of a lack of support in the company and he would not or rather could not actively perform as a pipeline with MITI.
8) The *wa* between MITI and the company would break

down, causing both to look bad in the circular society.
9) The mass media would harshly criticize the unsavory tie between MITI and the company.
10) The company president would have to step down with a token apology to the *seken* (people outside the company) for displaying dirty linen in public.

The consequences of not having conducted *nemawashi* would thus be disastrous. The circular structure of the Japanese society simply does not permit circularly minded people to allow things to be done triangularly, according to the spirit of pyramidal corporate organization. Of course, it occasionally happens that a decision is made on the authority of the president alone. But when such a decision is handed down as the order of the president, there is no company-wide upsurge of morale. And the heavy concentration of power in the center of corporate gravity can wreck the *wa* of the company, and the *wa* with yet another circular system that puts *wa* pressure on it.

A recent example was a Mitsukoshi scandal, the Japanese version of the American Bendex affair. Okada, the dictatorial president of 300-year-old Mitsukoshi, virtually destroyed the image of the prestigious department store because of his continued personal relationship with Ms. Takehisa, a business-minded woman, who, cashing in on her privileged position as his mistress, lived off the fat of the land, squeezing the profit out of the corporation. This incident is a classic example of how fragile the Japanese notion of *wa* is when a man at the top gets overly dictatorial. Lack of checks and balances and heavy concentration of power in the hands of one man is considered a weakness inherent in the circularly-run Japanese corporation.

I know of no other country where the leaders of a corporation and their subordinates are so emotionally dependent on and sensitive to each other as in Japan. It is not only in relationships with subordinates but with everybody around—above, below, and to the side—that one expends psychology in daily human relations. Unless this is done, *nemawashi* power cannot be brought

123

into play when a crisis occurs. Why?

Japan is a *natto* society. *Natto*, my pet analogy to explain the sticky nature of Japanese society, is fermented soybeans, which many Westerners find smelly, sticky, gooey, and peculiar tasting. *Natto*, though consisting of individual soy beans, is only called *natto* in its collective form. The Japanese, stuck together like soy beans, think collectively, act collectively, make decisions collectively, and solve problems collectively. And this, so many a Westerner feels, is the most baffling characteristic of the Japanese.

The thing which protects the *natto* from an outside enemy is its viscid string. The single fermented bean loses its group identity when the string is cut. Such a bean quickly decays and dies. It is like a kite whose guy string has been severed.

The way to get along in the *natto* society is to make use of the strings or simply develop them. *Giri* (moral obligation, a debt of gratitude) and *ninjo* (human feelings or heart) are manifestations of the strings. *Gyosei shido* (administrative guidance) is also part of the connecting string. The string has the power to protect individuals and corporations—and conversely to strangle them. Generally speaking, the men of real influence within the company are the generalists who, like *natto*, have enough strings or sticky contacts, and by no means the specialists who can demonstrate proven skills in their specialized area, but show no interest in networking.

Commonly used expressions among businessmen such as *hosu* (to bar a person from significant work), *murahachibu-ni suru* (to ostracize), and *shakaiteki-ni homuru* (to bury socially or professionally) all mean that a person is unilaterally cut off from the string. They are forms of punishment in the *natto* society.

Another characteristic of the string is that its effectiveness weakens with the passage of time. A matter of the greatest concern to a person assigned to an overseas post is the possibility of a break in the string between him and the head office. Physical distance and passage of time makes the *natto* people nervous and keeps them in constant fear. To the people of other countries, it seems that Japanese businessmen in overseas posts are working with their eyes turned to Tokyo and do not have their feet firmly on the ground.

As I have repeatedly mentioned, Japan is a circular society in which one feels most comfortable in the center and least comfortable at the periphery. Even a high-ranking executive who returns from an outside post to an inside post feels awkward at first. He finds himself an outsider surrounded by insiders even when faced by subordinates and cautiously addresses them with the honorific "san." After taking the subordinates out a few times to popular drinking houses (nawanoren), he starts to call them "kun" (a form of addressing lower-ranking, usually younger persons), and finally reaches the stage where he addresses them only by their surname without even adding the kun. By the time the kun stage is reached, the emotionally symbiotic relationship that exists only between and among insiders has been established between the addresser and the addressee. Thus nemawashi has worked. And another round of nemawashi will follow some other day to strengthen the emotional string.

Can nemawashi work in foreign-owned companies in Japan? Countless cases can be cited of employee morale being dampened and management efficiency being lowered because a Western manager disregarded nemawashi and issued a top-down command straight down the pecking order. In a natto corporation which brews amae (mutual dependence), employees, individual soy beans protected by the "wet" string, will not act voluntarily unless the proper method of stirring the natto with emotional chopsticks is carred out: nemawashi.

Having once been employed at a sogo shosha, a general trading firm, and then at the American Embassy as a simultaneous interpreter and then back to a Japanese financial company as an executive assistant, I consider myself qualified to cite crosscultural examples based on my experiences. The mistakes I made at the American Embassy included the one of "overstepping" my immediate supervisor to get what I wanted: streamlining communications within the Embassy. The affirmative action I took to bring the attention of the top management to the problem was construed as "surreptitious" and I was reprimanded by my immediate supervisor for having threatened his position. I didn't ignore him; I simply played a human relations game by the Japanese rules at an office where the game must be played by the rule of vertical movement. It was not until that time, when I was looked upon as a potentially dangerous person, that I realized that I had unconsciously played a game of "circularity" in my previous Japanese company, a game that enables one to work with anybody, anyplace, anywhere, irrespective of the spirit of organization, as long as one makes no mistakes in timing.

I fondly reminisced about the time when I was a "human," able to depend emotionally on my "human" corporate family. Colleagues are everywhere, members of the Judo Club, or of the English Speaking Circle, *senpai* (seniors) of my organization, or my section colleagues, each having his own human network that extends vertically, horizontally, or sideways depending on the type of relationship, called *en*: place of birth, school, or kinship. Within the Embassy, however, I felt like a tiny little cog in a huge "inhuman" machine. I felt I was an interpreting machine first, an interpreter second, a human third. Contrary to my initial opinion that the Embassy was a horizontal society because nobody, not even my master of simultaneous interpreting, called me Matsumoto *kun* (vertical) but *san* (horizontal), I learned the hard way that it is the American society that is intrinsically vertical. I suddenly got the urge to write about *haragei*.

In retrospect there was not a single *nemawashi* during my year-and-a-half stay with the Embassy. I am not saying my bosses had no *hara* but the vertical system of the Embassy did not permit them to show *hara*. My empathy goes to them now. The extra-logic of *hara* makes no distinction between self and others. This is exactly the logic of *natto*, and the opposite of *amanatto*, unsticky soy beans, which resembled the American Embassy as I personally saw and experienced it.

What moves the *natto* as a whole are not the individual soybeans but the strings. This can easily be observed if the *natto* is stirred with chopsticks. The quickest way to move the *natto* corporate family is to direct the chopsticks at middle management. It is invariably men of *hara* who are expected to take the role of chopsticks people-movers, during *nemawashi* in the close-knit and cohesive corporate climate.

How does *nemawashi* work in dealing with a foreign corporation? The first thing that should be undertaken, perhaps, is personal negotiation with the outside. This is *nemawashi* rule number 1. Sometimes, however, intra-company negotiations must come first. Which comes first depends on the merits of each situation.

The schemer wracks his brain trying to obtain intra-company consensus. If the project is suddenly broached at a meeting, it would only alienate the participants of the meeting. The nature of the project demands that *nemawashi* should begin within the department first. Personal negotiations should begin with the "insiders," then continue with other departments.

The *nemawashi* negotiation may start at a *yakitori* (grilled chicken) shop or a coffee shop and rise progressively to more expensive venues—popular drinking houses, bars, and first-class restaurants. As the rank of the object of *nemawashi* becomes higher, the meeting place becomes more expensive and the nature of the *nemawashi* becomes more sophisticated. *Nemawashi* experts are usually lavish entertainers and drinkers themselves. According to the National Tax Administration Agency, Japanese businessmen spend more on dining, wining, and gift buying than the whole country does on national defense. This proves that *nemawashi* is part of the business game in Japan. When the *nemawashi* meeting place reaches the level of high-class restaurants, the behind-the-scenes drama nears its climax.

Those who refuse to participate in the *nemawashi* held outside office hours at informal meeting places are labeled as disturbers of *wa*. They are discreetly shunted aside or removed from posts or even ordered to go on a business trip overseas for a hastily made up reason. These *persona non grata* become outsiders who are not allowed to participate in the ceremony. When the phonograph needle nears the center of the disc, the *nemawashi* is completed and the solemn ceremony begins, with all the insiders in, and outsiders out.

If the bottom-up *nemawashi* has gone this far, consensus reached is an offer the supreme decision-maker cannot refuse, unless he is extremely dictatorial. What is left for the chief executive officer to say to stop the music of the record is, "Has the *nemawashi* been completed?" The ceremonial *kaigi* (conference) follows the completion of the stage-setting. The ceremony proceeds without a hitch and the participants' breaths are met. No debate but *haragei*. The decision has already been made through the substantive give-and-take during *nemawashi* prior to the meeting. But the ritualistic recognition of the breathers' consensus is necessary to make sure that everyone has participated in the decision. Maybe what foreign corporate managers regard with envy about Japanese management is the high morale which comes from a sense of belonging and participation. *Nemawashi* brings people together on the same breathlength. If the merits and demerits of this circular system are analyzed logically, the merits would seem to far outnumber the demerits. As a practical matter, it is impossible to do away with *nemawashi*, since it is the product of Japan's psychological climate, which, in turn, is an outgrowth of a rice-growing culture.

3. *Haragei* as a positive-sum business game

"At first it seemed as if America was a paradise for management, but then I learned that even management can be fired. That came as a real shock." (Akio Morita's speech at the Kennedy School of Business)

There is a popular saying in Japan that goes *"Tada yori takai mono wa nai,"* meaning: "Nothing is more costly than something given free of charge." Strange, isn't it? Common sense tells us that what one wins is what others lose in zero-sum games. But not in Japan: where an individual identifies with the group first and with himself second, one must learn to play a positive-sum or an everybody-is-OK-and-therefore-I-am-OK game. This positive-and-varying-sum game is the game *haragei* performers are unconsciously playing. To play a zero-sum game, you must use your mind for a short-term orientation, but to play a positive-sum game you must use your heart as well for mid-term gains. And for a long-range undertaking, use your *hara*. The rationale behind this is that *hara*, being an embodiment of nature, must be everlasting in nature.

A businessman of *hara*, therefore, prefers to accept any demand as it comes and so says 'yes,' as nature does, and then asks his own *hara* to see if the demand is "natural" in consideration of payments for other employees. If his *hara* is set roughly at 100,000 yen for a piece of work done by a temporary worker, and the worker demands 200,000 yen for the job, he will say 'yes' and sign the contract for another year. If the worker demands 300,000 yen for the job, he will say 'yes' but this may be it. The contract will not be renewed. If 400,000 yen is demanded, his breathing may get a little shallower. But the payment will still be made with a smile without losing control of his *hara* as a balancer of his heart and mind. And then he smiles inwardly because he does not have to pay the worker a *sayonara* bonus he had had in his *hara* as a symbolic gesture of appreciation. The amount of bonus earlier intended will be split among those who had big enough *hara* not to demand anything. A man of *hara* is circumspect enough to hurt nobody's feelings. *Hara* by nature operates circularly, whereas mind works straight, heart erratically. This is why a boss who plays favorites with his employees may be in possession of hearts and minds but definitely lack *hara*. This particular businessman proved himself a man of *hara* by being sensitive not only to the person he was dealing with but also to those within his sphere of influence (circular). His *hara* is steadfastly 'yes,' but his mind or heart interpreting his *hara* message reacts differently to the varied demands made.

One of the most pleasing but toughest requests made of a man of *hara* is: "I'll leave it up to you." Upon hearing this, the business deal will continue uninterruptedly as long as mutual breathing does not get asymmetrical. This type of contract that is not spelled out is often referred to as *mokuyaku*, or "tacit contract."

A businessman of *hara* does not spell out the contract after having agreed in principle on a conceptual framework. Two men of *hara* in a business talk involving a contract will be kept busy reacting to each other's actions. The reason why Kansai businessmen are considered tough and shrewd is that they play one-upmanship more subtly than Kanto businessmen by the rule of *mokuyaku* (or tacit contract) based on *hara*-to-*hara* dealings.

A Kansai man's *hara* may operate like this: If a *ryokan* (inn) maid demands payment for a room service, the man simply offers her three choices: 5,000 yen, 10,000 yen, or 20,000 yen, and demands she pick one according to what she considers "natural" for the service she thinks she has rendered for him. She learns that it is insensitive of her to have acted rather than reacted. She blushes, feeling ashamed of having mentioned money, and remains awkwardly silent. This was a casual and yet for me an unforgettable scene in a situation drama on TV titled "Doterai Yatsu," based on the true story of a successful Kansai businessman who made it with wits and guts as well as heart and *hara*.

The moral of the story is that money is not something you demand but something that comes around to you in a circular way as a natural result of your service to the *seken* (the circle surrounding you). Money must be made circularly available and service must be circularly rendered in accordance with the law of nature, which is circular. The man proved himself a man of *hara* by subtly teaching the woman a lesson on *hara* ethics.

Konosuke Matsushita, adroit in displaying this sort of *hara*, successfully donated an overpass in front of the busy Hankyu Department Store. "Successfully," because everybody—including myself—who walks on the bridge feels *giri*-indebted to him for his big-*hara* action. Youths in the western half of Japan particularly idolize the management lord. What public relations art!

Hara is not taught at business schools. Harvard Business School boasts that 3,500 of its MBAs (Master of Business Administration) head U.S. corporations and they include 19% of the top three officers of the *Fortune* 500. The MBAs see themselves as the best and brightest. But viewing the declining productivity of the American economy, Akio Morita, chairman and co-founder of Sony, doesn't mince words: "For much of the trouble of the American economy, American management has to take the responsibility."

Time magazine's cover story entitled "The Money Chase" (May 4, 1981) makes this clear, listing what American business schools teach. Listed first is what is not taught.

1) They don't teach methods of handling people. They teach how to be bottom-line oriented through facts and figures.
2) They don't teach loyalty to their corporations. They teach how to be loyal to oneself.
3) They don't teach about the technology of producing goods. They teach about financial maneuvering.
4) They don't teach the importance of the development of international markets, like mergers and acquisitions.
5) They don't teach ethics. They simply teach how to define the area of responsibility.
6) They don't teach patience or humility. They teach independence.
7) They don't teach long-term planning and investment. They teach short-term profit.

In short, what is not taught at business schools in the United States is *hara*.

Long-term planning, to businessmen of *hara*, is a naturally enacted business practice. What is the link between long-term planning and *hara*? Here is *hara*-logical reasoning: A company must grow "organically." It must grow circularly rather than triangularly. It takes *hara* to treat a company as a whole "humanely" from a long-term perspective. A "humane" corporation wants to grow humanely as members of the corporate family do, as stressed in a bestseller, *In Search of Excellence*, citing attributes that make American companies excellent. Logic tears people and company apart; *hara*-logic brings them together. Logic tells us the money-losing programs must be scrapped, deadwood eliminated. *Hara*-logic tells us cutting off unprofitable programs or employees only hurts and bleeds the company.

If a foreign investor plans to do business in Japan, he must, first and foremost, invest in people. Business practice based on logic requires cutting back, and this is not restricted to commercial assets. People are also laid off. But in Japan businessmen invest with an eye for the future.

According to Douglas MacGregor's X-Y theory, there are two types of business managers. The theory-X manager says the carrot-and-stick policy is necessary because workers are by definition lazy and unreliable. The theory-Y manager, however, says that workers are ambitious and reliable. It may be going too far to see the former as rational and the latter as emotional, but that is essentially what it boils down to. One says you have to squeeze every drop of sweat out of them or they won't lift a finger. The other says if you keep your mouth shut and trust your workers, they will do as they should. The distance between them equals the distance between the mind and the heart. These two extremes must be synthesized by *hara*. The highly publicized *Theory Z* is nothing but a *hara* solution, nothing more and nothing less.

Let me explain briefly. By using the mind, business efficiency will improve. By using the heart, the overall sense of belonging increases, thus raising effectiveness. But by using the *hara*, both efficiency and effectiveness can be achieved. Prof. Richard Tanner Pascale states in *The Art of Japanese Management*: "The inherent preferences of organizations are clarity, certainty, and perfection. The inherent nature of human relationships involves ambiguity, uncertainty, and imperfection. How one honors, balances, and integrates the needs of both is the real trick of management."

The answer, in my opinion, lies in management's *hara*. X and Y are not mutually exclusive, but can be made complementary in a circular way. The extension of Y is X, which, in turn, is the extension of Y. The spiraling-inward process of mutual interaction between X and Y will eventually reach Z. *Hara*, as a balancer of X and Y, will enable the two to maintain a competitive-cooperative relationship for organic growth as in the figures below.

The business leader of *hara* who believes in the organic growth of his company will also expect his son to grow organically before he makes a decision to let his son step into his shoes. Torn between sending his son to an American business school to develop his mind and asking a friend if he could "use" his son as an unpaid executive driver or a janitor, to develop his *hara* through "under-

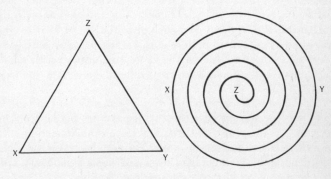

Figure 7   Triangle vs Circle

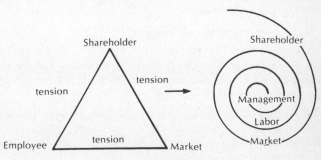

Figure 8   Triangle and Circle

dog" experience, the businessman of *hara* would pick the latter. The mind can better learn the figures; but *hara* can better understand people. As long as Japanese corporations remain, rightly or wrongly, people-centered and oriented toward circular (organic) growth, the circular *hara* will definitely take precedence over the triangular mind.

There are three interacting forces at work within a growth-minded American corporation: the forces known as "shareholder," "market," and "employee." (*Zen And Creative Management* by Albert Low) Assuming that American corporations feel more comfortable with the triangular interacting forces than with the circular notion of growth, and push on with their *idee fixe* even in Japan, something will definitely give. Let me prove this by using two symbols, the triangle vs. the circle, to come up with what I consider an ideal symbol of crosscultural corporate management.

These diagrams partly explain why Toyota's free gift of 25 trucks to the county of Los Angeles led triangular-thinking Americans to suspect that the Japanese automaker had an ulterior motive, and why American management based on the "cold" triangle does not work in Japan any more than a Japanese "warm" circle works in the United States unless modified to accommodate both shapes. In triangular societies, what one gains is what the other loses, whereas in circular societies, what one loses is what one gains eventually.

4. How to do effective *nemawashi*

In view of the fact that many successful businessmen associate *nemawashi* negotiations with *haragei*, the following twenty-three ground rules for *nemawashi* may be of help for the foreign businessmen on the outside looking in.

1. Consider situations (time, place, and occasion) over principles.
2. Start working with less influential and yet "proper" figures one at a time.
3. Constantly develop your human network.
4. Work behind the scenes on your scenario.

5. Organize your thoughts before persuading others, but be prepared to change them if the situation so demands.
6. Hang tough in person-to-person dealings. (Enthusiasm and sincerity count more than technique.)
7. Market your *hara* (long-term commitment) first, your product second.
8. Let others talk so that they find themselves involved in the project.
9. Get an early start to give *nemawashi* time to grow.
10. Prepare thoroughly and don't overlook the follow-up.
11. Try to be cheerful, meticulous, and considerate of others' needs.
12. Try not to badmouth others behind their backs.
13. Develop your contacts in your informal circle away from your formal circle.
14. Size up the person's *hara* rather than his mind or heart for strategy, while trying hard to read into the person's *hara* for tactics.
15. Increase the number of interpersonal contacts rather than playing games skillfully.
16. Let your righthand man do *nemawashi* for you while making yourself as unobtrusive as possible.
17. Fool insiders first, outsiders second, if the matter is of a highly confidential nature.
18. Let others get the message by subtly dropping hints.
19. Try not to over-win in negotiations. Remember the *hara-gei* axiom: to win is to lose.
20. Let others subtly realize you are carrying a big stick, and look prepared to swing it when the chips are down.
21. Be patient and ready to eat crow when you must.
22. Treat heavy matters lightly and light matters heavily (part of the samurai code of ethics).
23. Come up with the non-arguable slogan "*taigimeibun*" (for the sake of . . .), or the group-serving principle, to serve the situation.

V

DOES *HARAGEI* HAVE
A FUTURE?

A. *Haragei* and computers

Debate, an extension of Greek *syllogistic* reasoning, is considered
a rational means of problem-solving and decision-making as well
as of scientific discovery; whereas circular *haragei*, its opposite,
unproductive and unconstructive by nature, has been considered
an unscientific or non-dialectic means of "harmonizing" with
problem areas. There is no reason why *haragei* should not endeav-
or to "harmonize" with debate to find more imaginative and
yet *holistic* solutions to our future problems, through the crossover
marriage that produces an eventual "synergistic effect." Debate
may not be able to define *haragei*, as proven previously; *haragei*
could define debate. It may symbolize the growing spiritual ties
between Zen Buddhism, which assumes the mind (or heart) and
body are one, and Christianity, which places the mental above the
physical.

Triangle and Circle. East and West. Can the twain meet in the
future? Yes, and they must.

Under the facade of the advancement of medical science, men
in the East and the West have been permitted to explore the mys-
teries of human brains, gene-splicing, organ-transplanting, and
even blood-type transferring. Ironically, just at the time when
people began to play God, robots began to play humans. Japan,

the world's largest manufacturer of industrial robots, should seriously consider ways and means of living with those robots. The so-far innocent cohabitation of humans and robots will surely run the risk of leading to a "love suicide" if and when the robots, an extension of our body, begin to demand emotional participation in human activities.

How far have we come since Hippocrates located the seat of the intellect inside the skull 2,400 years ago? Everyone knows that emotions come from within the brain, although no one knows yet how they arise. It is true that recently neuroscientists are beginning to suspect that it is a mere interaction of chemicals and electricity inside the brain that makes us human. It is also true, according to *Newsweek*, February 7, 1983, that scientists are coming to realize that the brain is less a collection of isolated little players, each responsible for a different melody in the mental symphony, than a unified orchestra, with small numbers of neurons conducting an ensemble of millions.

The above *Newsweek* cover story quotes Dr. Daniel Weinberger of the National Institute of Mental Health as saying, "A lot of old theories about right brain and left brain are nonsense." This accelerating rate of advancement of medical science might eventually demythologize the "uniqueness" of the Japanese brain. Even so, I doubt if science could locate the exact position of *hara*, much less the chemistry between *hara* and other parts of the brain.

Yes, machines will get smarter, becoming more and more human. It may not be too long before they will be able to reason, argue or negotiate efficiently—eventually outperforming us humans.

A long as a man becomes more like a machine and a machine becomes more like a man in the forthcoming computer generation, man will eventually lose out to machine in a battle between computers and human biocomputers. Robots, no matter how sophisticated, do not need a coffee break, they do not demand a raise, they do not have to be fed, clothed, stroked, or punished. How serious, then, would their threat be to modern men in general? Computers can be honest, logical, realistic, intelligent, and friendly to men. Put into Skinnerian boxes, they could be better disciplined and better behaved than men.

But can they contradict themselves? Can they breathe? Based on the assumption that straight logic is inherent in computer thinking and contradictions are an inalienable right of human beings, *haragei*, with its innate power of self-contradiction, can be one of man's impregnable fortresses against the computer threat. Technically, computers are not and will not be capable of *haragei*. They cannot be fitted with *hara*. Morally, computers should not do *haragei*. Computers should remain principled. With the advent of microkids in the computer generation, more and more people will gravitate toward computer (binal) thinking: true or false, friends or enemies, push the button or don't push the button (as in the movie *War Games*), thus further "dehumanizing" their thinking.

If there is only one thing that will save the world from nuclear holocaust, it is not the mind, which creates the poles of "yes" and "no," but the *hara*, which accepts both "yes" and "no," both guilty and not guilty, and both inside and outside as mutually inclusive. More precisely, it is not the kind of love that you develop in your mind or heart, because the mind-heart love can be won or lost on human initiative; it is the absolute love (or *hara*-love) that grows naturally inside everyone's *hara*, born of nature, because only *hara*-love, through its ecological instinct, knows how to "stomach" both friends and enemies and both animate and inanimate beings as one and the same.

In view of the increasing invasion by computers of the domain of human activities, modern man will feel compelled to think in opposition to computer thinking: thinking in *hara*. It is not in spite of, but because of, the increased demands of computer thinking that we as eventual programmers must rely on *hara*-thinking, or what Don Juan calls our "body-knowing," to experience reality that lies beyond words. Inasmuch as breathing remains a proof of human reality, there should be no reason why *haragei*, an art of synchronized breathing or a means of achieving a "growing up together" of ideas, should not be encouraged across national boundaries and culture lines, in whatever form it presents itself outside Japan. *Haragei* must survive.

B. Conclusion

During the course of my *haragei* expedition, I have encountered two major schools of thought: those who argue that *haragei* is the monopoly of the Japanese and those who argue that *haragei* is not unique to Japan.

The former believe that emphasis on similarities is neither fun nor informative, while the latter believe that excessive focus on cultural differences is hazardous for intercultural communication. Logic tells us that, other than the fact that both arguments are instinctive and emotional, they are mutually exclusive.

But *hara*-logic tells us they are complementary, since similarities and dissimilarities are each other's extension in a circular way. Man of circular *hara* can be what Peter S. Adler calls multicultural man, who can transcend the boundaries of nationalism and ethnocentrism while committed to a vision of the world as a global community. I do not remember how many times I have debated triangularly or argued circularly with my friendly devil's advocates, Japanese and non-Japanese, to come up with the renewed notion of intercultural *haragei* as it should be; neither do I recall how many times for the past ten years I have thought of giving up writing this book because of the conflict with my original faith that *haragei* should belong to Japan. In retrospect, in times of emotional stability I have relied on my mind, but under enormous stress, say while defining value-free *hara* and its art, I have resorted to my trump card: my *hara*. It helps me expand my mind beyond myself. Why? Ask Karlfried Dürckheim. And he will eloquently describe *hara* as a connecting link between being beyond space and time, and our existence in space and time.

The original purpose of my discussion of *haragei* (a center-to-center communication) was to stress the uniqueness of *haragei* and the mentality of the Japanese who set such high store on *hara* and *gei*, but the logic of the situation has forced me to change the earlier objective of my writing from being "centripetal"—to Japan as an axis of the universe—to being "centrifugal"— away from the center to the rest of the world. Is this a sell-out on my part? Hardly. And I am not sorry that I have contradicted myself. I have changed my *hara*. The centripetal force coiled inside my *hara* seems to have gotten the better of the otherwise-centrifugal inclination in me and has moved me outward to the rest of the world. The *hara* did it. Mine? Or yours?

EPILOGUE

Foreign observers, particularly intellectuals, wonder aloud if the Japanese can truly understand the meaning of questions that begin with Why? or What If?—seemingly the cornerstone of risk management thinking. The notion of risk, however is a recent development in Japan where there is an old saying that goes, "think about tomorrow and the devil will laugh at you." This leads many a foreign visitor to conclude that the Japanese may make excellent "crisis managers" but rarely good "risk managers." Otherwise stated, the difference between crisis aversion know-how and "what would we do if this happened" risk thinking is great among Japanese.

How, then, would Japanese go about managing crises and avoiding risks? How unique would Japanese crisis management be if put into an international perspective?

Let me try a simulation exercise with the reader as a means of identifying the possible behavioral patterns that vary from one race to another, employing an oft-used hypothetical situation, carried somewhat to absurdity, involving a woman and two males who find themselves far from civilization's knowing eyes.

The following might be laughed away as another silly little ethnic joke, but at the risk of being labeled a racist or sexist, I venture to convey with exaggerated examples some kernel of truth to prove that each culture *gets the kind of crisis management it deserves*.

On a tropical desert island, under the shadow of a palm tree lies a woman (nationality unknown) of ordinary beauty. Two males drift ashore. What might happen?

American males:
The average American male *calculates risk* first, of say contracting a social disease. An average American is an American who

141

does not know the meaning of average and only speaks for himself or herself. The two American males would maintain a cautious distance from her. This, after all, is an isolated example.

British Males:

British males do not consider it very sporting to attain her without a show of valor and sportsmanship. They believe in sportsmanlike decision making. So they fight a duel over the woman, risking their lives for the decision.

French Males:

Born and brought up in a *no risk involved atmosphere*, they seem to have no problem establishing rapport with the woman and getting along among the three of them. Free love or grape-picking? The suave French males simply blame it on the ambience of the particular situation.

German Males:

The ordnung (order) prohibits them from violently befriending the woman so the two argue loudly with each. They do not debate specifics; they debate the fundamentals. Why is the woman there? Shouldn't the woman be given the option to manage the crisis caused by these two male latecomers? They are too carried away to touch the woman. And they are not above carrying their verbal confrontation into a physical conflict, once out of the country of order, as is often the case with other nationals.

Italians males:

The jovial Italian males do not see it as a crisis; they see it as an opportunity. The absence of wine gives them no choice but to dance and sing boisterously to seduce the woman into their families. Italians, minus the phlegmatic mafia, believe in flowery gestures and inflated words for their purposes.

Chinese Males:

They, Yin and Yang, engage in a symbolic verbal boxing using symbolic pronouns with political implications, say Mozart, before approaching the woman. When the polemics are over, absolute silence returns. Mr. Yin is excused and swims away from the shore. Mr. Yang nears her with a broad country smile and seeks her company. The woman spends a night with Mr. Yang and learns when the sun is up next morning that she had been sleeping with Mr. Yin instead of Mr. Yang. Nobody knows what happened along the way much less why.

Male orthodox Jews:

They violently exchange why-because arguments between them but never get into a fist fight. They go to the Bible (Old Testament). A. presents a case that they should not commit adultery. B. counter-argues that being out on a no man's land this is an extenuating circumstance.

Then they go to the Talmud and read it until either one uses situational logic to come up with a third case that says they should abandon their Jewish identity and faith to avoid being punished by Jewish laws or anti-Semitism. The result: They assimilate into her identity. If marrying does not work . . . they buy her out.

Japanese Males:

Perplexed by a situation they have yet to confront, they first send a telex to their home office in Tokyo informing them of the "unprecedented" event. They then ponder a method of avoiding the potential crisis lest it threaten their group harmony in the name of *"Kyodai Jingi"* (Emotional bondage between brothers). They do not argue. They simply exchange poetic messages between them, because everything is understood by them at the level of each other's *hara*. The younger, by the name of Mr. *Kohai* gives Mr. *Sempai* (his elder or superior) an option with a bow and smile. No conflict. Mr. *Sempai* keeps the woman company, but soon gets uncomfortable because his *hara* is being sized up. The real crisis sets in when Mr. *Sempai* learns that the woman loves Mr. *Kohai* (his junior) more than she loves him. Mr. *Sempai* does not want to lose face for losing the woman and worse still for making Mr. *Kohai* think he has caused his superior to lose face. Both of them must devise face-saving outs for the other.

Mr. *Sempai* feels compelled to behave like a *Sempai* (senior) or prove himself an *oyabun* (masculine boss) through the demonstration of *hara* in front of his junior. It takes *haragei* to manage the situation. Mr. *Sempai* after seemingly having had fun with the woman, pretends to sleep, giving his subordinate a chance to be alone with her.

Embraced by the sense of security nurtured by Japan's time-honored *jingi* and yet under social pressure, neither of the males can "go all the way" with the woman with whom they are face-bound to maintain a polite distance. Neither is physically satisfied. But then neither gets the AIDS virus. All this shows how potential crises can be nipped in the bud by the elders' subtle *haragei*.

Serious discussions of *haragei* are sometimes logical, sometimes not. When you try to understand *haragei*, do so not with your mind or your heart, but with your *hara*.

BIBLIOGRAPHY

Benedict, Ruth. *The Chrysanthemum and the Sword*, Tuttle, Tokyo, 1954

Berne, Eric. *Games People Play*, Ballantine Books, New York, 1978

Butow, Robert. *Japan's Decision to Surrender*, Stanford University Press, Stanford, Cal., 1954

Capra, Fritjof. *Tao of Physics*, Bantam Books, New York, 1975

Castaneda, Carlos. *Separate Reality*, Pocket Books, New York, 1971

Conklin, Robert. *How to Get People to Do Things*, Contemporary Books, Chicago, 1979

Doi, Takeo. *The Anatomy of Dependence*, Kodansha International, Tokyo, 1973

Dürckheim, Karlfried. *Hara; The Vital Centre of Man*, Mandala Books, Unwin Paperbacks, London, 1977

Hall, Edward. *The Hidden Dimension*, Anchor Books, New York, 1969

Harris, Thomas. *I'm OK-You're OK*, Avon Books, New York, 1967

Herrigel, Eugen. *Zen in the Art of Archery*, Random House, New York, 1971

Imai, Masaaki. *Never Take Yes for an Answer*, Simul Press, Tokyo, 1975

Low, Albert. *Zen and Creative Management*, Playboy Paperbacks, New York, 1976

Matsushita, Konosuke. *Thoughts on Man*, PHP Institute International, Tokyo, 1981

Miyoshi, Masao. *As We Saw Them*, University of California Press, Berkeley, Cal., 1979

Nitobe, Inazo. *Bushido*, Tuttle, Tokyo, 1967

Pascale, Richard & Athos, Anthony. *The Art of Japanese Management*, Simon & Schuster, New York, 1981

Peters, Thomas & Waterman, Robert Jr. *In Search of Excellence*, Harper & Row, New York, 1982

Suzuki, Daisetz. *Zen and Japanese Culture*, Princeton U Pr, Princeton, New Jersey, 1959

Taylor, Jared. *Shadows of the Rising Sun*, William Morrow, New York, 1983

Trevanian. *Shibumi*, Ballantine Books, New York, 1979

Whiting, Robert. *The Chrysanthemum and the Bat*, Permanent Press, Tokyo, 1977

Yamaoka, Haruo. *Meditation Gut Enlightenment: The Way of Hara*, Heian Intl., San Francisco, Ca., 1976.

INDEX

Neighborhood Tokyo

Theodore C. Bestor

A glimpse into the everyday lives, commerce, and relationships of some two thousand neighborhood residents living in the heart of Tokyo.

The Book Of Tea

Kazuko Okakura
Foreword and Afterword by Soshitsu Sen XV

A new presentation of the seminal text on the meaning and practice of tea—illustrated with eight historic photographs.

Geisha, Gangster, Neighbor, Nun

Donald Richie

A collection of highly personal portraits of Japanese men and women—some famous, some obscure—from Mishima and Kawabata to a sushi apprentice and a bar madame.

Womansword
What Japanese Words Say About Women

Kittredge Cherry

From "cockroach husband" to "daughter-in-a-box"—a mix of provocative and entertaining Japanese words that collectively tell the story of Japanese women.

The Compact Culture
The Japanese Tradition of "Smaller is Better"

O-Young Lee/Translated by Robert N. Huey

A long history of skillfully reducing things and concepts to their essentials reveals the essence of the Japanese character and, in part, accounts for Japan's business success.

Acts of Worship Seven Stories
Yukio Mishima/Translated by John Bester

These seven consistently interesting stories, each with its own distinctive atmosphere and mood, are a timely reminder of Mishima the consummate writer.

Sun and Steel
Yukio Mishima/Translated by John Bester

This fascinating document—part autobiography, part reflections on the search for personal identity—traces Mishima's life from an introverted childhood to a creative maturity.

The House of Nire
Morio Kita/Translated by Dennis Keene

A comic novel that captures the essence of Japanese society while chronicling the lives of the Nire family and their involvement in the family-run mental hospital.

Requiem
Shizuko Gō/Translated by Geraldine Harcourt

A best seller in Japanese, this moving requiem for war victims won the Akutagawa Prize and voiced the feelings of a generation of Japanese women.

A Cat, a Man, and Two Women
Jun'ichiro Tanizaki/Translated by Paul McCarthy

Lightheartedness and comic realism distinguish this wonderful collection—a novella (the title story) and two shorter pieces. The eminent Tanizaki at his best.

Child of Fortune
Yuko Tsushima/Translated by Geraldine Harcourt

Awarded the Women's Literature Prize, *Child of Fortune* offers a penetrating look at a divorced mother's reluctant struggle against powerful, conformist social pressures.

BEST SELLING TITLES
NOW AVAILABLE IN PAPERBACK

Literature

THE DOCTOR'S WIFE
Sawako Ariyoshi/Translated by Wakako Hironaka & Ann Siller Kostant
"An excellent story."—*Choice*

THE LAKE
Yasunari Kawabata/Translated by Reiko Tsukimura
By Japan's only Nobel Prize–winning author.

POINTS AND LINES
Japan's Best-Selling Mystery
Seichō Matsumoto/Translated by Makiko Yamamoto & Paul C. Blum

THE RELUCTANT ADMIRAL
Yamamoto and the Imperial Navy
Hiroyuki Agawa/Translated by John Bester

MATSUO BASHŌ
The Master Haiku Poet
Makoto Ueda

ALMOST TRANSPARENT BLUE
Ryu Murakami/Translated by Nancy Andrew
"A Japanese mix of *Clockwork Orange* and *L'Etranger*."—
Newsweek

THE DAY MAN LOST
Hiroshima, 6 August 1945
The Pacific War Research Society

THE HAIKU HANDBOOK
How to Write, Share, and Teach Haiku
William J. Higginson with Penny Harter
Available only in Japan.